CREATION AND
RE-CREATION

Sandra L. Taylor

Order this book online at www.trafford.com
or email orders@trafford.com

Most Trafford titles are also available at major online book retailers.

Printed in the United States of America.

ISBN: 978-1-4269-3839-9 (sc)
ISBN: 978-1-4269-3841-2 (e)

Library of Congress Control Number: 2010911117

*Our mission is to efficiently provide the world's finest, most comprehensive
book publishing service, enabling every author to experience success.
To find out how to publish your book, your way, and have it available
worldwide, visit us online at www.trafford.com*

Trafford rev. 08/23/2010

www.trafford.com

North America & international
toll-free: 1 888 232 4444 (USA & Canada)
phone: 250 383 6864 ♦ fax: 812 355 4082

THIS BOOK IS DEDICATED TO

My sister, Carol and my brother, John, for it was because of you that I was inspired to write this book;

My children, Michael, Nancy and Jill, for the love and support you have given me;

My Grandchildren, Matthew, Sarah, Rachel, Christopher, Brandon, Ridge and Kennedy to whom the truths in this book will one day be very valuable;

And last, but certainly not least, to people everywhere who need answers to questions about salvation.

TO GOD BE THE GLORY FOR HIS WORD!

The cover for this book was drawn by Chelsa Richardson, who presently resides on Texas Death Row for Women. God has gifted her with amazing talent to draw while in constant pain in her wrist every day. Chelsea has accepted Jesus as her Savior and has been forgiven for her past. She has found eternal life with Jesus now. Read how you too can have that eternal life with Jesus.

FOREWORD

At this time in history there has been increasing Biblical illiteracy. Even the Christian world has been lacking in the understanding of what salvation really means. Just knowing about Jesus and attending a church doesn't save a person. It is important to have an understanding of the foundational truths that are in the Bible, as well as knowledge of God's plan for mankind.

Many people, even in the churches of today, have never been taught the foundational message of salvation and the need of a Savior. This book shows the foundational truths of what the Bible teaches about the sin nature and the need for a Savior for every person born since the beginning of time as we know it.

I am very impressed with the substance of this book and the clarity with which it was presented. I particularly like the way Sandra explains the fall of man and the subsequent plan of redemption that God provides for all who will receive it. This is a good book for someone to read who needs to understand how man was created and what happened from the time God created man until the present day.

This book is a good foundational message for new believers to use as a study guide to the Bible. It is also a good book to remind believers of what Jesus has done for them. This is a great tool to lead others to the saving knowledge of Jesus Christ and how to be born again.

This is a book whose time has come.

Pastor Gloria Gillespie
Lighthouse Church
Burleson, Texas

THE BUTTERFLY

Such a beautiful creature, the butterfly! The life of the butterfly is so like the born again experience we have when we accept Jesus as our Savior.

The butterfly starts out as a lowly little caterpillar. The caterpillar is confined to the earth or at best to a twig of a tree. He crawls around at a slow pace, searching for food and trying not to be eaten by the birds or other predators. Some caterpillars are cute and fuzzy, while others are smooth- skinned and not much to look at.

The caterpillar reminds me of those who have not been born again. We all start out in life as a caterpillar . . . searching, trying to make it through this life here on earth. We are always aware of the predators who want to devour us in some way. Some of us are nice looking and some not so nice looking on the outside. We don't know what we are searching for, but we know that somewhere out there is that something that will fill that empty void inside.

Something miraculous happens to the caterpillar, however. Once he has grown to his full potential, he finds a good solid twig and begins to spin a cocoon around himself. Then he dies to his old caterpillar body. In fact, his body completely liquefies.

But his death is only the beginning of a wonderful new life. By some miraculous act of God, his body begins to form into a new shape and he is born again. He takes on the form of a beautiful butterfly. Once he is fully formed into the butterfly, he emerges from the cocoon (not without a struggle) into the world again.

The person who accepts Jesus into his or her life has somewhat the same experience Once we have come to a certain place in life (usually one where we can no longer go on as we are) we call upon God and ask Jesus to come into our heart. We die to our old ways and become new creations in Christ Jesus. We usually struggle along the way to understand what this new life is all about, but we begin to see things through the eyes of our Creator now. It is a whole new world to us.

The butterfly no longer has to crawl on the ground or a twig. It can now fly above it all. It is free to flitter from flower to flower and to enjoy its new life from above the things on the ground.

That is the way it is when we become born again into the kingdom of God. We can now understand His word to us in the Bible. We can see things from above the circumstances.

That is why this book was written. As you read it, you will see things from God's perspective according to what His word means. You can go from a caterpillar to a butterfly, from creation to re-creation in Christ Jesus our Lord and Savior.

Welcome to the world of the butterfly!

TABLE OF CONTENTS

INTRODUCTION

HOW DID THIS UNIVERSE GET HERE? WHERE DID THE EARTH, THE SUN, THE MOON, THE STARS AND THE PLANETS COME FROM? WHERE DID WE COME FROM? DID IT ALL JUST SUDDENLY COME INTO EXISTENCE? DID IT ALL EVOLVE INTO EXISTENCE?

SCIENCE HAS GIVEN US NO ADEQUATE REASON FOR THE UNIVERSE.

THERE HAVE BEEN MANY THEORIES, BUT AS MAN GAINS MORE KNOWLEDGE, HE CHANGES HIS THEORIES.

TRUTH NEEDS NO REVISION. YET, THEORIES ARE CONTINUALLY REVISED, AND OFTEN TIMES ARGUED ABOUT, WITH NO SOLUTIONS.

AS FAR AS OUR SCIENTISTS KNOW, THE EARTH IS THE ONLY PLANET WITH LIFE ON IT. ACCORDING TO SCIENCE, THERE ARE THREE KINDS OF LIFE: ANIMAL LIFE, VEGETABLE LIFE

AND HUMAN LIFE. SO, HOW DID LIFE COME INTO BEING?

TO SAY THAT THERE IS NO CREATOR OF ALL OF THIS IS TO SAY THAT IT DOESN'T EXIST. BUT, IT DOES EXIST! SO, THERE MUST BE A GREAT MASTER-MIND THAT CREATED IT ALL.

OF COURSE THERE IS! THERE CAN BE NO OTHER EXPLANATION. THERE IS A GOD WHO CREATED EVERYTHING. IF NOT, THEN WHY CAN'T OUR GREAT SCIENTISTS AGREE AND EXPLAIN IN ACTUALITY AND IN TRUTH, WITH NO REVISIONS, JUST HOW IT GOT HERE?

MAN CONTACTS THE UNIVERSE THROUGH HIS FIVE SENSES. BUT WHAT MAKES MAN LIVE? IT CAN'T BE THE HEART, THE BLOOD OR THE BRAIN; WHEN MAN DIES, THAT ALL STAYS INSIDE OF HIS BODY.

WHAT ABOUT DEATH ANYWAY? WHAT REALLY HAPPENS WHEN MAN DIES? IS THERE LIFE AFTER DEATH?

THE FACT IS THERE IS ANOTHER FORM OF LIFE BESIDES THE ANIMAL, VEGETABLE AND HUMAN LIFE THAT SCIENCE RECOGNIZES. THERE IS SPIRITUAL LIFE, WHICH IS WHAT GIVES LIFE TO ALL CREATION.

A PERSON NEVER REALLY DIES! HIS LIFE GOES SOMEWHERE ELSE!

SO WHO IS GOD? WHAT IS HIS NAME? IS HE A GOD OF WRATH OR IS HE REALLY A GOD OF LOVE AS SO MANY WHO BELIEVE IN HIM SAY? IF THERE REALLY IS A GOD, AND HE DOES LOVE US, WHY ARE THERE SO MANY TERRIBLE THINGS HAPPENING IN THE WORLD? WHY DO WE HAVE WARS? WHY CAN'T PEOPLE GET ALONG WITH EACH OTHER? WHY ARE SOME PEOPLE ON EARTH STARVING AND DYING, LIVING IN POVERTY AND WANT, WHILE OTHERS ARE SO RICH THEY COULD NEVER SPEND IT ALL IN A LIFETIME? WHY WERE WE BORN INTO THIS LIFE, ONLY TO BE SO MISERABLE, SICK AND UNHAPPY MOST OF THE TIME?

FOR MOST OF US, THE QUESTIONS GO UNANSWERED. NOW AND THEN WE HEAR ABOUT GOD, ABOUT A SAVIOR, BUT WE EITHER REJECT HIM OR WE CAN'T UNDERSTAND, SO WE CAST THE THOUGHTS ASIDE OR PUT THE BIBLE BACK ON THE SHELF, AND WE GO ON WONDERING --- WHY?

ONE THING IS CERTAIN. IN EACH AND EVERY PERSON ON THIS EARTH, WITHOUT EXCEPTION, THERE IS A LONGING TO BE COMPLETE, TO BE AT PEACE, TO HAVE EVERYTHING GOOD, WONDERFUL AND PERFECT IN OUR LIFE.

THE FACT REMAINS, HOWEVER, THAT THERE IS AN EMPTY PLACE IN EACH ONE OF US. <u>SOMETHING INSIDE IS LACKING</u>! NO MATTER HOW MUCH WE LONG FOR THAT COMPLETENESS AND FULFILLMENT WITHIN, NO MATTER HOW MUCH FAME AND FORTUNE WE ACQUIRE, THE VOID, EMPTINESS AND CRAVING FOR "SOMETHING MORE" IS STILL THERE. WHY? WHAT IS LACKING?

RATHER THAN SPECULATE, LET'S SEARCH FOR THE ANSWERS TO SOME OF OUR QUESTIONS. THE ONLY WAY WE CAN DO THAT, IS TO SEEK THE ANSWERS WITH AN OPEN MIND, WANTING TO KNOW THE TRUTH RATHER THAN WHAT WE HAVE BEEN TOLD, OR WHAT WE THINK THE ANSWERS SHOULD BE. ALL MAN EVER WANTS TO KNOW IS WHAT THE TRUTH REALLY IS. NO ONE LIKES TO BE DECEIVED.

BUT, WHO HAS THE TRUTH? WHERE DO WE FIND TRUTH?

THERE IN ONLY ONE WHO HAS THE ANSWERS TO MAN'S QUESTIONS THE ONE WHO CREATED MAN AND THE UNIVERSE. SO, LET US ASK GOD, HIMSELF.

THERE IS ONE AGELESS BOOK THAT GIVES THE ANSWERS TO ALL OF MAN'S QUESTIONS. IT IS THE BIBLE. THE BIBLE HAS BEEN GIVEN TO MANKIND BY OUR CREATOR, GOD. IN

THE BIBLE LIE A MULTITUDE OF PRECIOUS
TRUTHS AND EXPLANATIONS FOR ALL OF OUR
QUESTIONS. SO, LET'S FIND OUT WHAT THE
BIBLE IS REALLY ALL ABOUT.

WHAT IS THE BIBLE?

EVERY BOOK HAS A MESSAGE OR STORY OR A REASON FOR BEING WRITTEN, BE IT FACT OR FICTION. THOSE BOOKS WHICH HAVE A SUBJECT TO DISCUSS, A MESSAGE TO PORTRAY, OR A LESSON TO TEACH ARE WRITTEN BY AUTHORS WHO HAVE THE KNOWLEDGE NECESSARY TO WRITE THEM.

THE BIBLE IS NO EXCEPTION. "ALL SCRIPTURE IS INSPIRED BY GOD, AND PROFITABLE FOR TEACHING, FOR REPROOF, FOR CORRECTION FOR TEACHING IN RIGHTEOUSNESS." (II TIMOTHY 3:16)

"FOR NO PROPHECY WAS EVER MADE BY AN ACT OF HUMAN WILL, BUT MEN MOVED BY THE HOLY SPIRIT SPOKE FROM GOD." (II PETER 1:21)

"FOR WHATEVER WAS WRITTEN IN EARLIER TIMES WAS WRITTEN FOR OUR INSTRUCTION, THAT THROUGH PERSEVERANCE AND THE ENCOURAGEMENT OF THE SCRIPTURES WE MIGHT HAVE HOPE." (ROMANS 15:4)

SO, WE SEE THAT THE BIBLE IS THE INSPIRED <u>WORD OF GOD</u> SPOKEN THROUGH HIS PROPHETS FOR OUR INSTRUCTION SO WE CAN PERSEVERE AND HAVE ENCOURAGEMENT. BY READING THE SCRIPTURES CONTAINED IN THE BIBLE WE CAN HAVE HOPE TO UNDERSTAND ALL THOSE QUESTIONS WE HAVE. THE AUTHOR OF THE BIBLE IS GOD, HIMSELF.

WHY IS IT THEN THAT WHEN WE SIT DOWN TO READ IT, IT MAKES NO SENSE TO US? WHY CAN'T WE UNDERSTAND IT?

SINCE ALL THE ANSWERS TO OUR QUESTIONS ARE CONTAINED IN THE BIBLE. LET US ASK THE ONE WHO WROTE IT---GOD, HIMSELF.

HIS ANSWER IS FOUND IN JOHN 3:1-5

"NOW THERE WAS A MAN OF THE PHARISEES, NAMED NICODEMUS, A RULER OF THE JEWS; THIS MAN CAME TO HIM BY NIGHT, AND SAID TO HIM, 'RABBI, WE KNOW THAT YOU HAVE COME FROM GOD AS A TEACHER; FOR NO ONE CAN DO THESE SIGNS THAT YOU DO UNLESS GOD IS WITH HIM.' JESUS ANSWERED AND SAID TO HIM, 'TRULY, TRULY, I SAY TO YOU, UNLESS ONE IS BORN OF THE WATER AND THE SPIRIT, HE CANNOT SEE THE KINGDOM OF GOD.' NICODEMUS SAID TO HIM, 'HOW CAN A MAN BE BORN WHEN HE

IS OLD? HE CANNOT ENTER A SECOND TIME INTO HIS MOTHER'S WOMB AND BE BORN, CAN HE?' JESUS ANSWERED, 'TRULY, TRULY, I SAY TO YOU, UNLESS ONE IS BORN OF WATER AND THE SPIRIT, HE CANNOT ENTER INTO THE KINGDOM OF GOD."

NICODEMUS WAS A RULER OF THE JEWS. HE KNEW THE LAWS GIVEN TO MOSES AND ALL THE LAWS REQUIRED BY GOD IN ORDER TO CLEANSE AND SANCTIFY THE PEOPLE SO THAT GOD COULD ACCEPT THEM BECAUSE OF THE SINFULNESS IN THE WORLD. JESUS CAME TEACHING A NEW MESSAGE, AND NICODEMUS WAS PUZZLED BECAUSE IT WAS SO DIFFERENT FROM THE OLD LAW GOD HAD GIVEN IN MOSES' TIME. IT WAS A MESSAGE GIVEN BY THE AUTHORITY OF GOD THROUGH JESUS TO TEACH MEN. IT WAS BACKED UP BY SUPERNATURAL SIGNS AND WONDERS, AND NICODEMUS KNEW THAT "NO ONE CAN DO THESE SIGNS (OR MIRACLES) THAT YOU DO UNLESS GOD IS WITH HIM." (VS 2)

THE ANSWER JESUS GAVE NICODEMUS IS THE SAME ANSWER TO THE QUESTION, "WHY CAN'T I UNDERSTAND THE BIBLE?" JESUS SAID, "TRULY, TRULY, I SAY TO YOU, UNLESS ONE IS BORN AGAIN HE CANNOT SEE (OR UNDERSTAND) THE KINGDOM OF GOD." (VS 3)

SO, WHY CAN'T WE UNDERSTAND THE BIBLE? LET US READ WHAT GOD'S WORD SAYS. "BUT THEIR MINDS WERE HARDENED; FOR UNTIL THIS VERY DAY AT THE READING OF THE OLD COVENANT THE SAME VEIL REMAINS UNLIFTED, BECAUSE IT IS REMOVED IN CHRIST." IN OTHER WORDS, YOU MUST BE BORN AGAIN IN ORDER TO SEE IT! "BUT TO THIS DAY WHENEVER MOSES (THE BIBLE) IS READ, A VEIL LIES OVER THEIR HEART; BUT WHENEVER A MAN TURNS TO THE LORD, THE VEIL IS TAKEN AWAY." (II CORINTHIANS 3:14-16) MAN CANNOT UNDERSTAND IT UNLESS HE TURNS TO THE LORD. THEN GOD, HIMSELF, WILL TAKE THE VEIL AWAY.

"IN WHOSE CASE THE GOD OF THIS WORLD HAS BLINDED THE MINDS OF THE UNBELIEVING, THAT THEY MIGHT NOT SEE THE LIGHT OF THE GOSPEL OF THE GLORY OF CHRIST, WHO IS THE IMAGE OF GOD." (II CORINTHIANS 4:4)

IF YOU CHOOSE TO NOT WANT TO KNOW ANYTHING ABOUT GOD AND HIS WORD, YOU ARE AN UNBELIEVER. AS AN UNBELIEVER, YOU CANNOT UNDERSTAND THE BIBLE BECAUSE YOUR MIND IS BLOCKED. YOU MUST AT LEAST CHOOSE TO STUDY IT FOR YOURSELF. THEN GOD WILL OPEN HIS WORD TO YOU.

WE WILL SEE LATER WHAT IT MEANS TO BE BORN AGAIN AND WHO THE GOD OF

THIS WORLD IS. OUR FIRST PRIORITY MUST BE TO UNDERSTAND THE BIBLE AND WHAT IT HAS TO SAY ABOUT CREATION AND THE UNIVERSE. WE MUST ESTABLISH SOME FACTS VERY FIRMLY IN OUR MINDS BEFORE WE GO ON WITH MORE QUESTIONS, LEST WE ARE LED ASTRAY BY WHAT MEN SAY AND TEACH OR BY WHAT WE THINK RATHER THAN WHAT GOD HAS TO SAY ABOUT IT.

ABOVE ALL ELSE, PLEASE ESTABLISH IN YOUR HEART AND MIND THAT YOU MUST READ, STUDY AND BELIEVE WHAT THE BIBLE, GOD'S WORD, SAYS AND NOT WHAT YOU HEAR OR HAVE HEARD OR HAVE BEEN TAUGHT.

THE MAJORITY OF THE MINISTERS AND PROPHETS OF TODAY DO NOT TEACH THE TRUTH AS IT IS IN GOD'S WORD. THEY TEACH THE DOCTRINES AND THEOLOGIES OF MEN BEFORE THEM. THEY TEACH HEARSAY AND VISIONS OR DREAMS OF OTHER MEN -- NOT THE BIBLE.

MANY TEACH WHAT THEY ARE TOLD TO TEACH BY THEIR PARTICULAR CHURCH, BE IT DENOMINATIONAL OR NON-DENOMINATIONAL. GOD, BY HIS SPIRIT IS NOT ALLOWED TO MOVE IN MOST CHURCHES TODAY. MAN HAS HIS PROGRAM AND IT MUST BE FOLLOWED ON SCHEDULE, ACCORDING TO HIS PLAN, ACCORDING TO WHAT HIS KNOWLEDGE IS, NOT GOD'S

GOD'S WORD ALSO STATES VERY CLEARLY THAT "EVERY FACT IS TO BE CONFIRMED BY THE TESTIMONY OF TWO OR THREE WITNESSES." (II CORINTHIANS 13:1; MATTHEW 18:16; DEUTERONOMY 19:15)

THEREFORE, IN SEEKING ANSWERS TO OUR QUESTIONS FROM GOD, WE MUST HAVE TWO OR THREE WITNESSES IN HIS WORD -- NOT FROM PEOPLE (EVERYONE CAN ALWAYS FIND AT LEAST ONE OR TWO PEOPLE TO AGREE WITH THEM IF THEY LOOK LONG ENOUGH). BUT ACCORDING TO THE WORD OF GOD, WE MUST HAVE AT LEAST TWO OR MORE PLACES IN THE WORD OF GOD, THE BIBLE, TO VERIFY EACH SCRIPTURE. THIS IS THE WAY THAT GOD SET HIS WORD BEFORE US. THIS IS HIS WAY OF CONFIRMING HIS WORD TO US. **IF IT ISN'T IN HIS WORD, DO NOT BELIEVE IT**!!

YOU CAN ALREADY SEE BY THESE QUOTES FROM THE BIBLE THAT THERE ARE REASONS WHY WE HAVE BEEN UNABLE TO UNDERSTAND GOD AND HIS CREATION.

SO, AS WE SEEK THE ANSWERS TO OUR QUESTIONS, LET US REMEMBER WHAT WE HAVE LEARNED SO FAR:

1. ALL SCRIPTURE IS THE INSPIRED WORD OF GOD.

2. ALL SCRIPTURE WAS SPOKEN THROUGH HIS PROPHETS FOR OUR INSTRUCTION AND ENCOURAGEMENT.

3. WE MUST BE BORN AGAIN IN ORDER TO SEE OR UNDERSTAND IT.

4. THE GOD OF THIS WORLD HAS BLINDED US -- BUT WHENEVER A MAN TURNS TO THE LORD, THE VEIL IS TAKEN AWAY, AND GOD HIMSELF OPENS HIS WORD UP TO HIM.

5. WE MUST STUDY AND BELIEVE WHAT GOD'S WORD SAYS.

6. EVERY FACT IS TO BE CONFIRMED BY TWO OR THREE WITNESSES IN GOD'S WORD.

AS YOU STUDY THIS TEACHING, ASK GOD TO SHOW YOU THE TRUTH. DILIGENTLY SEEK HIM. HE WILL LIFT THE VEIL!

THE SCRIPTURES USED IN THIS STUDY WILL BE TAKEN FROM THE NEW AMERICAN STANDARD VERSION OF THE BIBLE, EXCEPT WHERE NOTED AS COMING FROM A DIFFERENT VERSION.

CAN WE UNDERSTAND THE MYSTERIES OF GOD?

MANY PEOPLE AND MANY THEOLOGIANS TODAY SAY, "WE CAN'T UNDERSTAND THE MYSTERIES OF GOD." BUT WE CAN'T LISTEN TO THEM. WHAT DOES THE BIBLE SAY?

GOD'S WORD STATES VERY CLEARLY, "FOR NOTHING IS HIDDEN EXCEPT TO BE REVEALED, NOR HAS ANYTHING BEEN SECRET BUT THAT IT SHOULD COME TO LIGHT." (MARK 4:22; MATTHEW 10:26; LUKE 8:17; LUKE 12:2) "FOR WHATEVER WAS WRITTEN IN EARLIER TIMES WAS WRITTEN FOR OUR INSTRUCTION..." (ROMANS 15:4). "ALL SCRIPTURE IS INSPIRED BY GOD AND PROFITABLE FOR TEACHING, FOR REPROOF, FOR CORRECTION, FOR TRAINING IN RIGHTEOUSNESS." (II TIMOTHY 3:16) "...NO PROPHESY OF SCRIPTURE IS A MATTER OF ONE'S OWN INTERPRETATION, FOR NO PROPHECY WAS EVER MADE BY AN ACT OF HUMAN WILL, BUT <u>MEN MOVED BY THE HOLY SPIRIT SPOKE FROM GOD</u>." (II PETER 1:20—21)

JESUS SAID TO HIS DISCIPLES WHO WERE WITH HIM AT THE TIME, THE SAME THING AS HIS WORD SAYS TO THE DISCIPLES WHO FOLLOW HIM TODAY..."TO YOU IT HAS BEEN GRANTED TO KNOW THE MYSTERIES OF THE KINGDOM OF HEAVEN." -AND- "TO YOU HAS BEEN GIVEN THE MYSTERY OF THE KINGDOM OF GOD, BUT THOSE WHO ARE OUTSIDE GET EVERYTHING IN PARABLES." (MARK 4:11; MATTHEW 13:10-11; LUKE 8:10)

THE WORD OF GOD IS FULL OF MYSTERIES WHICH MAN IN HIS NATURAL MIND CANNOT UNDERSTAND. JESUS SPOKE TO THE MULTITUDES AND PEOPLE HE TAUGHT IN PARABLES. SOME SAY A BIBLE PARABLE IS AN EARTHLY STORY WITH A HEAVENLY MEANING. WEBSTER'S DICTIONARY DEFINES A PARABLE AS A SHORT SIMPLE STORY WITH A MORAL LESSON AND IS USUALLY AN ALLEGORY. AN ALLEGORY IS A STORY IN WHICH PEOPLE, THINGS AND HAPPENINGS HAVE ANOTHER MEANING, OFTEN MORALLY INSTRUCTIVE. SO, IF WE PUT IT ALL TOGETHER, A BIBLE PARABLE IS A STORY TOLD TO THE NATURAL MINDS OF MEN, BUT WITH A MORAL, HEAVENLY, SPIRITUAL MEANING. IT HAS A FAR DIFFERENT MEANING THAN WHAT MAN'S MIND CAN COMPREHEND. **IN FACT, MAN MUST BE BORN AGAIN IN ORDER TO UNDERSTAND IT.**

TO WHOM ARE THE MYSTERIES OF GOD REVEALED? TO HIS DISCIPLES! **TO THOSE WHO**

ARE BORN AGAIN. TO THEM IT HAS BEEN GRANTED TO KNOW THE MYSTERIES OF THE KINGDOM OF GOD; BUT TO THE OTHERS, IT HAS NOT BEEN GRANTED. TO THOSE WHO HAVE NOT BEEN BORN AGAIN, GOD SPEAKS IN MYSTERIES AND PARABLES.

SO WE CAN KNOW THE MYSTERIES OF GOD. GOD'S WORD SAYS WE CAN. THIS WILL COME AS A SHOCK TO MOST OF THE CHURCH-GOING PEOPLE OF TODAY . . . BUT THE BIBLE ISN'T FOR THE UNBORN-AGAIN MAN. THE BIBLE CANNOT BE UNDERSTOOD OR EXPLAINED APART FROM HAVING THE VEIL LIFTED. MAN CANNOT LEARN FROM MAN THE MYSTERIES OF GOD APART FROM THE TRUTH OF GOD'S WORD; AND THE TRUTH OF GOD'S WORD IS NEVER REVEALED TO THE UNBORN-AGAIN MAN.

THAT VEIL IS LIFTED ONLY BY FOLLOWING GOD'S WORD AND, LAYING A FOUNDATION OF TRUTH IN THE SPIRIT OF MAN. ONCE THE FOUNDATION IS LAID ACCORDING TO HIS WORD, GOD WILL LIFT THE VEIL HIMSELF. GOD REQUIRES MAN TO READ AND OBEY HIS WORD.

OUR FATHER, GOD IS ABLE TO ESTABLISH THE TRUTH AND REVEAL HIS MYSTERIES TO US. HE HAS GIVEN US ALL THE ANSWERS WE NEED IN THE BIBLE, WHICH IS HIS WORD TO US. THROUGH THE PROPHETS AND SAINTS

THAT WERE BEFORE US, HE HAS MADE KNOWN HIS MYSTERIES WHICH LEAD US TO OBEDIENCE BY FAITH IN HIM AND IN HIS SON, JESUS CHRIST.

WHAT IS THE REASON FOR CREATION?

"IN THE BEGINNING GOD CREATED THE HEAVENS AND THE EARTH." (GENESIS 1:1)

"AND GOD CREATED MAN IN HIS OWN IMAGE, IN THE IMAGE OF GOD HE CREATED HIM; MALE AND FEMALE HE CREATED THEM. AND GOD BLESSED THEM; AND GOD SAID TO THEM, 'BE FRUITFUL AND MULTIPLY, AND FILL THE EARTH AND SUBDUE IT; AND RULE OVER THE FISH OF THE SEA AND OVER THE BIRDS OF THE SKY, AND OVER EVERY LIVING THING THAT MOVES ON THE EARTH.'" (GENESIS 1:26-27)

THERE IS A VAST AMOUNT OF KNOWLEDGE AND REVELATION IN THE FIRST TWO CHAPTERS OF THE BIBLE. THE BOOK OF GENESIS GIVES US AN ACCOUNT OF HOW THE EARTH, THE HEAVENS AND MAN REALLY GOT HERE. IF YOU HAVE A BIBLE, PLEASE READ GENESIS 1 AND 2.

GOD CREATED THE HEAVENS AND ALL THAT IS IN THEM. HE CREATED THE SUN, THE MOON, THE PLANETS, THE STARS AND THE GREAT EXPANSE THAT THE SCIENTISTS CONTINUE TO DISCOVER.

GOD CREATED THE EARTH AND ALL THAT IS IN IT AND ON IT. HE CREATED THE ANIMAL LIFE AND THE VEGETABLE LIFE. HE CREATED EVERYTHING FROM THE SMALLEST MINUTE CELL TO THE LARGEST GIGANTIC MOUNTAIN.

THEN, GOD CREATED MAN IN HIS IMAGE AND LIKENESS. STOP AND THINK ABOUT THAT FOR A MOMENT. **MAN WAS CREATED IN THE IMAGE OF GOD! MAN WAS MADE JUST LIKE GOD**! PSALMS 8:5 SAYS MAN WAS CREATED A LITTLE LOWER THAN ELOHIM. ELOHIM MEANS GOD; SO, IT MEANS MAN WAS CREATED A LITTLE LOWER THAN GOD!

THEN, GOD GAVE MAN DOMINION OVER ALL THE EARTH. HE WAS GIVEN AUTHORITY OVER EVERYTHING ON THE EARTH. GOD TOLD HIM TO SUBDUE THE EARTH AND MULTIPLY AND FILL THE EARTH. GOD MADE IT ALL, AND THEN GAVE IT TO MAN AS HIS OWN POSSESSION.

"AND GOD SAW ALL THAT HE HAD MADE, AND BEHOLD, IT WAS VERY GOOD." (GENESIS

1:31) GOD SAID THAT IT WAS "GOOD" NOT EVIL. IT WAS PERFECT.

DID YOU KNOW THAT SCIENTISTS HAVE DISCOVERED THAT EACH PLANET AND EACH STAR HAVE BEEN PERFECTLY PLACED SO THAT THE EARTH WILL NOT GO OUT OF ORBIT? EACH HEAVENLY CREATED THING HAS BEEN PLACED WITH GRAVITATIONAL PULL TO KEEP THE EARTH ON ITS COURSE.

SCIENTISTS ALSO DISCOVERED LONG AGO THAT THE EARTH WILL VENTURE OUT OF ORBIT EVERY SO MANY YEARS. HOWEVER, THEY NOTICED THAT A COMET ORBITS THE EARTH DURING THAT TIME AND APPEARS JUST AT THE PROPER TIME TO PULL THE EARTH BACK ON COURSE AGAIN.

THAT IS HOW PERFECTLY GOD CREATED THIS UNIVERSE. THIS UNIVERSE WAS CREATED FOR THE EARTH; THE EARTH WAS CREATED FOR MAN AND WAS GIVEN TO MAN TO RULE AND CARE FOR.

WHY ISN'T THE EARTH STILL PERFECT?

READING GENESIS CHAPTER 1, WE SEE WHAT GOD DID. GENESIS CHAPTER 2 TELLS US HOW GOD DID IT AND WHAT WAS EXPECTED OF MAN IN ORDER TO KEEP THE DOMAIN GOD GAVE TO HIM.

"GOD IS A SPIRIT". (JOHN 4:24) MAN WAS CREATED IN GOD' S IMAGE AND LIKENESS. SO, MAN WAS CREATED A SPIRIT BEING. GOD HAS A MIND, WILL AND EMOTIONS. MAN HAS A MIND, WILL AND EMOTIONS. GOD GAVE MAN A MIND OF HIS OWN AND A WILL OF HIS OWN. HE ALLOWED MAN TO CHOOSE FOR HIMSELF.

GOD IS THE FATHER OF MAN. HE GAVE LIFE TO MAN. AS OUR FATHER, HE DIDN'T WANT PUPPETS. HE WANTED MAN TO LOVE HIM AND TALK AND COMMUNE WITH HIM. HE WANTED CHILDREN, LIKE ANY HUMAN FATHER WANTS CHILDREN. THE DESIRES WE HAVE IN US AS PARENTS, ARE THE SAME

DESIRES GOD HAS. WE HAVE BEEN CREATED IN HIS IMAGE.

GENESIS CHAPTER 2 BEGINS WITH A VERY INTERESTING STATEMENT:

"THUS, THE HEAVENS AND THE EARTH WERE FINISHED." GOD ENDED HIS WORK ON THE SEVENTH DAY, AND HE RESTED FROM ALL THE WORK HE HAD DONE. **HE GAVE IT TO MAN TO CARE FOR**.

GENESIS 2:15 SHOWS THAT GOD PUT MAN IN A GARDEN CALLED EDEN.

EDEN MEANS "PARADISE". THE BIBLE STATES THAT MAN WAS TO GUARD AND KEEP THIS GARDEN. GOD HAD PROVIDED MAN'S EVERY NEED IN THAT GARDEN AND MAN WAS PERFECT. THERE WAS NO DISEASE IN HIM, NO EVIL IN HIM, AND HE WAS CLOTHED WITH THE GLORY OF GOD, TO THE POINT WHERE HE NEEDED NO OTHER CLOTHING. HE WAS A SPIRITUAL BEING JUST LIKE GOD.

GENESIS 2:16-17 SHOWS THAT GOD GAVE MAN A CHOICE. GOD TOLD HIM THAT HE COULD EAT OF ANY TREE IN THE GARDEN OF EDEN EXCEPT THE TREE OF THE KNOWLEDGE OF GOOD AND EVIL. HE WARNED HIM THAT IN THE DAY HE ATE OF IT, HE WOULD SURELY DIE.

THEN GOD DECIDED IT WAS NOT GOOD FOR THE MAN TO BE ALONE. HE GAVE THE AUTHORITY TO MAN TO NAME EVERYTHING ON THE EARTH. WHATEVER THE MAN, ADAM, CALLED A THING, THAT WAS ITS NAME.

THERE WAS NO ANIMAL THAT COULD BE COMPATIBLE WITH ADAM. HE WAS THE ONLY LIVING BEING CREATED IN GOD'S IMAGE AND NOTHING BUT A BEING CREATED IN GOD'S IMAGE WOULD BE ABLE TO BE A HELPER OR COMPANION SUITABLE FOR ADAM.

HERE IS AN INTERESTING REVELATION. GOD CAUSED ADAM TO SLEEP AND TOOK OUT OF ADAM THE FEMALE PART OF HIM AND BROUGHT HER TO HIM. SINCE MAN IS MADE IN THE IMAGE OF GOD, GOD MUST HAVE BOTH MALE AND FEMALE IN HIM.

GOD IS OUR FATHER, WITH ALL THE ATTRIBUTES OF THE POWER, STRENGTH AND LOVE OF THE MALE. HE IS ALSO OUR MOTHER, WITH ALL THE ATTRIBUTES OF TENDERNESS, LOVE AND COMPASSION OF THE FEMALE.

ADAM NOW HAD THE MALE ATTRIBUTES, AND EVE HAD THE FEMALE ATTRIBUTES. WITHOUT EACH OTHER, THEY WERE NOT COMPLETE. ADAM CALLED HER BONE OF HIS BONE AND FLESH OF HIS FLESH AND NAMED HER WOMAN, BECAUSE SHE WAS TAKEN OUT OF MAN. THEY WERE TO BECOME ONE FLESH

IN ORDER TO BE COMPLETE IN THE IMAGE OF GOD.

GOD HAD ALSO CREATED HEAVENLY BEINGS. THE OLD TESTAMENT TELLS OF CHERUBIM, SERAPHIM AND ANGELS. SEVERAL PLACES IN THE OLD AND NEW TESTAMENT ANGELS HAVE BEEN SENT TO EARTH WITH MESSAGES FROM GOD TO MAN.

GOD ALSO CREATED A DEVIL. "I CREATED THE DESTROYER TO RUIN." (ISAIAH 54:16) THE KING JAMES VERSION OF THE BIBLE SAYS, "I CREATED THE WASTER TO DESTROY." JOHN 8:44 SAYS, "THE DEVIL WAS A MURDERER FROM THE BEGINNING." I JOHN 4:8 SAYS, "THE DEVIL HAS SINNED FROM THE BEGINNING."

WHY DID GOD CREATE THE DEVIL? SO THAT MAN COULD HAVE A CHOICE! IN THE GREAT PLAN OF GOD, MAN WAS TO LOVE AND FELLOWSHIP WITH GOD OUT OF HIS OWN WILL, BY HIS OWN CHOICE. GOD HAD TO PROVIDE A TEMPTER OF MANKIND IN ORDER FOR MAN TO CHOOSE.

THE DEVIL, ALSO KNOWN AS SATAN, HAS ATTRIBUTES TOTALLY THE OPPOSITE OF GOD. GOD'S NATURE IS LOVE AND LIFE. SATAN'S NATURE IS HATE AND DEATH. SATAN'S NATURE IS TO "KILL, STEAL AND DESTROY" (JOHN 10:10) GOD'S NATURE IS LIFE, LOVE, PEACE AND PROSPERITY.

THE BIBLE CALLS SATAN "A LIAR AND THE FATHER OF LIES. HE HAS NO TRUTH IN HIM." (JOHN 8:44) HE IS A DECEIVER, A TEMPTER OF MANKIND, A THIEF AND A MURDERER. HE HATES MANKIND AND EVERYTHING THAT GOD CREATED. HE HAS TRIED TO DESTROY IT SINCE THE DAY HE WAS CREATED.

IN GENESIS CHAPTER 3, WE SEE THE DEVIL COME IN THE FORM OF A SERPENT TO TEMPT EVE. HE ASKS HER A QUESTION ... "INDEED, HAS GOD SAID YOU SHALL NOT EAT FROM ANY TREE OF THE GARDEN?" (GENESIS 3:1)

THEN HE TELLS HER A LIE ... "YOU SHALL SURELY NOT DIE." (GENESIS 3:4)

GOD HAD SAID, "IN THE DAY YOU EAT OF IT, YOU SHALL SURELY DIE." (GENESIS 2:17) **WHAT GOD SAYS IS THE WAY IT WILL BE, WHETHER MAN BELIEVES IT OR NOT**.

LET US SEE WHAT EVE REALLY DID. FIRST OF ALL, SHE <u>LISTENED</u> TO WHAT THE DEVIL SAID. THEN SHE <u>LOOKED</u> AT THE TREE AND SAW THAT IT WAS GOOD TO LOOK AT. THEN SHE <u>THREW OUT</u> WHAT GOD HAD SAID AND <u>BELIEVED</u> THE DEVIL'S LIE THAT IT WOULD MAKE HER WISE. THEN SHE TOOK SOME OF THE FRUIT FROM THE FORBIDDEN TREE AND ATE IT.

PEOPLE DO THE SAME THINGS TODAY. THEY <u>LISTEN</u> TO EVERYTHING BUT GOD'S WORD. THEY <u>LOOK</u> AT THE THINGS THAT ARE OPPOSITE TO GOD'S WORD, THINKING THEY ARE GOOD TO LOOK AT AND ARE BETTER THAN WHAT GOD SAYS. THEY <u>THROW OUT</u> GOD'S WORD AND <u>BELIEVE</u> THE LIES OF THE DEVIL, THINKING THEY ARE WISER THAN GOD'S WORD.

MANY THINK THAT EVE WAS THE WHOLE CAUSE OF THE FALL OF MAN.

BUT, THE BIBLE TELLS US A DIFFERENT STORY. WHEN SHE ATE OF THE FRUIT OF THE TREE OF THE KNOWLEDGE OF GOOD AND EVIL, SHE GAVE SOME TO ADAM WHO WAS <u>WITH HER</u>. (GENESIS 3:6)

EVE WAS DECEIVED BY SATAN. BUT, ADAM, WHO HAD BEEN GIVEN THE COMMAND BEFORE EVE WAS CREATED, <u>WAS RIGHT THERE WITH HER</u>.

HE DIDN'T STOP HER. IN FACT, THE BIBLE DOESN'T RECORD THAT HE EVER SAID ANYTHING. NOT ONLY THAT, HE ATE OF THE FRUIT TOO!

<u>THAT IS THE REASON WHY THINGS ARE THE WAY THEY ARE TODAY!</u>

ADAM WILLFULLY CHOSE TO EAT AND TO DISOBEY GOD. NOT ONLY DID HE DISOBEY GOD, BUT <u>IN HIS DISOBEDIENCE, HE GAVE THE EARTH TO SATAN TO RULE OVER</u>. ADAM AND EVE DIED SPIRITUALLY THE MOMENT THEY ATE AND DISOBEYED GOD. GOD HAD SAID THAT IN THE DAY THEY ATE OF THAT TREE, THEY WOULD SURELY DIE. THEIR BODIES LIVED AND THEIR SOULS LIVED, BUT THEY WERE NO LONGER ALIVE TO GOD SPIRITUALLY.

THEY DIED SPIRITUALLY, AND WERE SEPARATED FROM GOD SPIRITUALLY FROM THAT DAY ON. THAT IS WHAT DEATH IS. IT IS PERMANENT, <u>ETERNAL</u> SEPARATION FROM GOD.

MANKIND IS COMPRISED OF THREE PARTS. HE IS A SPIRIT, HE HAS A SOUL AND HE LIVES IN A BODY. HIS BODY IS FORMED FROM THE DUST OF THE EARTH. (GENESIS 2:7) HIS SOUL POSSESSES HIS INTELLECT OR MIND, HIS WILL AND HIS EMOTIONS. HIS SPIRIT IS THE LIFE THAT GOD GIVES HIM UPON CONCEPTION.

ADAM AND EVE BOTH HAD THEIR MINDS OPENED TO GOOD AND EVIL.

THEY LOST THE GLORY OF GOD AS THEIR CLOTHING, AND THEY KNEW THEY WERE BOTH NAKED.

BEFORE THEY ATE OF THE TREE OF THE KNOWLEDGE OF GOOD AND EVIL, THEY KNEW ONLY THE PERFECT WILL OF GOD. GOD CAME AND WALKED AND TALKED WITH THEM. (GENESIS 3:8) HE WAS THEIR FATHER. HE LOVED THEM WITH A PERFECT LOVE, A LOVE WE CANNOT EVEN COMPREHEND. HE MUST HAVE GIVEN THEM GODLY KNOWLEDGE AND WISDOM. THEY HAD NO OTHER KNOWLEDGE EXCEPT WHAT GOD HAD GIVEN THEM. IMAGINE THE WONDERFUL COMMUNION THEY HAD WITH GOD, THE CREATOR OF THE UNIVERSE.

AFTER THEY ATE, THE NATURE OF SATAN ENTERED THEM. HIS NATURE IS SIN, DEATH AND DESTRUCTION. THEIR MINDS WERE NO LONGER PURE. THEY COULD NO LONGER LIVE IN THE REALM OF GOD. THEY BECAME DEAD TO SPIRITUAL THINGS. THEY COULD NO LONGER COMMUNE WITH THEIR FATHER, GOD.

THE BIBLE SAYS THEY KNEW SHAME. IMMEDIATELY AFTER THEY ATE, THEY SAW THAT THEY WERE NAKED AND TRIED TO SEW FIG LEAVES TOGETHER TO COVER THEMSELVES. (GENESIS 3:7)

WHEN THEY HEARD GOD WALKING IN THE GARDEN, THEY HID FROM HIM. FEAR HAD ENTERED THEM. THEY HAD NOT KNOWN FEAR BEFORE THAT. (GENESIS 3:8-10)

WHEN GOD QUESTIONED THEM, ADAM BLAMED EVE AND EVE BLAMED THE SERPENT. THEY LIED. THEY HAD NEVER DONE THAT BEFORE. (GENESIS 3- 11-13)

THE BIBLE DOESN'T MAKE IT CLEAR AS TO WHAT THE FRUIT OF THE TREE OF THE KNOWLEDGE OF GOOD AND EVIL WAS. MEN HAVE DECIDED IT WAS AN APPLE. BUT IT COULDN'T HAVE BEEN AN APPLE. IF IT WAS AN APPLE, THEN EVERY TIME WE ATE AN APPLE, WE WOULD CONTINUE TO GET THE KNOWLEDGE OF GOOD AND EVIL. WHATEVER IT WAS, IT OPENED THEM UP TO THE ABILITY TO RECEIVE EVIL THOUGHTS AND THE NATURE OF SATAN.

MAN IS STILL IN THIS CONDITION TODAY. WE HAVE THE FALLEN SIN NATURE THAT ADAM AND EVE HAD. THAT IS WHY WE HAVE SHAME, FEAR, IMPURITY, CORRUPTION AND ALL MANNER OF EVIL. WE ARE SPIRITUALLY SEPARATED FROM GOD AND SUBJECT TO DEATH.

GOD COULDN'T JUST "ZAP" SATAN AND CHANGE MAN BACK. MAN HAD LEGALLY CHOSEN TO DISOBEY GOD AND GIVE HIS DOMINION OVER THE EARTH TO SATAN. **BECAUSE GOD IS PERFECT, AND ABSOLUTELY JUST, HE HAD NO LEGAL RIGHT TO THE EARTH. HE HAD GIVEN IT TO MAN TO DO WITH AS HE PLEASED.**

FROM THAT TIME UNTIL TODAY, SATAN HAS HAD DOMINION OVER MAN AND THE EARTH. HE IS CALLED "THE GOD OF THIS WORLD". (II CORINTHIANS 4:4) HIS NATURE IS SEEN IN MEN, WOMEN AND CHILDREN TODAY WHO DO NOT KNOW GOD. DESTRUCTION AND CORRUPTION OF EVERY KIND IS CLEARLY SEEN IN ALL THE EARTH.

THERE WAS ONLY ONE WAY THAT GOD COULD REDEEM MAN OUT OF THE HAND OF SATAN AND GIVE MAN A CHOICE ONCE AGAIN TO FOLLOW GOD.

GOD HAD TO COME TO EARTH HIMSELF AS A PERFECT MAN, AND LIVE A SINLESS LIFE, NOT ALLOWING SATAN TO CAUSE HIM TO FALL LIKE ADAM DID.

SINCE SATAN IS THE RULER OF DEATH DUE TO MAN'S DISOBEDIENCE, GOD HAD TO TAKE MAN'S PLACE AND DIE IN HIS PLACE IN ORDER TO JUSTLY REDEEM MAN BACK FROM SATAN AND BACK INTO FELLOWSHIP WITH GOD.

THAT IS EXACTLY WHAT HE DID! BEFORE WE CAN LEARN HOW GOD DID THIS, WE MUST FIRST REALIZE THAT THE CONDITION MANKIND IS IN IS THE RESULT OF ADAM'S CHOICE. WE MUST DISCOVER FOR OURSELVES THE SERIOUSNESS OF OUR CONDITION AND THE CONSEQUENCES OF A DECISION NOT TO

BELIEVE IN GOD AND HIS WORD. SO, LET US LOOK AT WHAT THE BIBLE HAS TO SAY TO US TODAY.

WHO IS THE GOD OF THIS WORLD?

IN ORDER TO ANSWER THIS QUESTION, WE MUST DETERMINE WHAT THE BIBLE IS TALKING ABOUT WHEN THE WORD "WORLD" IS USED.

IN JOHN 8:23, JESUS WAS TALKING TO THE JEWS AND HE MADE A STATEMENT WHICH EXPLAINS THE WORD "WORLD". HE SAID, "YOU ARE FROM BELOW, I AM FROM ABOVE; YOU ARE OF THIS WORLD, I AM NOT OF THIS WORLD."

FURTHER SEARCHING OF THE SCRIPTURES REVEALS MORE EXPLANATION OF OUR QUESTION. "THE GOD OF THIS WORLD HAS BLINDED THE MINDS OF THE UNBELIEVING THAT THEY MAY NOT SEE THE LIGHT OF THE GOSPEL OF THE GLORY OF CHRIST, WHO IS THE IMAGE OF GOD." (II CORINTHIANS 4:4) "NOW JUDGMENT IS UPON THIS WORLD; NOW THE RULER OF THIS WORLD SHALL BE CAST OUT." (JOHN 12:31)

IT IS VERY PLAIN THAT JESUS WAS DESCRIBING THE REALM WE LIVE IN AS THE "WORLD", AND THAT HE WAS NOT OF THIS WORLD (OR REALM). HE SAID THE GOD OF THIS WORLD HAD BLINDED THE MINDS OF THE UNBELIEVING, AND THAT THE RULER OF THIS WORLD WOULD BE CAST OUT.

BY THESE SCRIPTURES, IT IS OBVIOUS THAT JESUS IS NOT THE GOD OF THIS WORLD (THE ONE THAT FALLEN MAN LIVES IN). JUDGMENT CAME UPON ALL MANKIND AND THE EARTH DUE TO THE FALL OF ADAM, BUT GOD SENT HIS SON, JESUS, TO OVERCOME SATAN, TO CAST HIM OUT AND TO RETURN THE WORLD BACK TO US TO RULE ONCE AGAIN.

WE NEED TO ESTABLISH ONE FACT BEFORE WE GO ON. **SATAN IS REAL! HIS BEST DECEPTION IS TO KEEP MANKIND BELIEVING THAT HE DOESN'T EXIST!**

IF WE DO DISCOVER THAT HE EXISTS, THEN HE TRIES TO GET US TO BELIEVE IN HIM RATHER THAN IN GOD. IF WE WON'T BELIEVE IN HIM, HE TRIES TO PLAY DOWN THE IMPORTANCE OF BELIEVING IN GOD, HOPING TO DECEIVE US INTO NOT PURSUING THE TRUTH... GETTING US TO THINK IT REALLY ISN'T ALL THAT IMPORTANT ANYWAY.

REMEMBER! ADAM GAVE THIS WORLD TO SATAN. <u>SATAN IS THE GOD OF THIS WORLD.</u>

HE RULES THE WORLD THAT WE SEE, THE REALM OF THE SENSES (SEEING, HEARING, TASTING, TOUCHING AND SMELLING). BECAUSE OF SATAN, WE ARE UNABLE TO SEE THE SUPERNATURAL, SPIRITUAL REALM WHICH IS THE **REAL WORLD**.

GOD IS A SPIRIT AND MAN WAS ORIGINALLY CREATED IN THE IMAGE OF GOD AS A SPIRIT BEING. BEFORE ADAM TURNED IT OVER TO SATAN, HE SAW THE REAL WORLD--THE SPIRIT WORLD.

SATAN HAS BLINDED ALL PEOPLE ON EARTH, MAKING THEM SUBJECT TO HIM, CAUSING THEM TO LIVE IN THE CORRUPTION WE SEE TODAY.

THE WORD OF GOD SAYS, "AND YOU WERE DEAD IN YOUR TRESPASSES AND SINS, IN WHICH YOU FORMERLY WALKED ACCORDING TO THE COURSE OF THIS WORLD, ACCORDING TO THE PRINCE OF THE POWER OF THE AIR, OF THE SPIRIT THAT IS NOW WORKING IN THE SONS OF DISOBEDIENCE." (EPHESIANS 2:1-2) EVERY MAN, WOMAN, AND CHILD BORN SINCE ADAM IS SPIRITUALLY DEAD IN SINS AND TRESPASSES, AND SUBJECT TO SATAN'S POWER.

ONLY IF WE TURN TO GOD, CAN WE ESCAPE SATAN'S POWER!

THE FACT IS THERE IS A DEVIL. GOD CREATED HIM. THERE IS ALSO A HELL. GOD ALSO CREATED HELL. HELL WAS CREATED FOR THE DEVIL AND HIS ANGELS. (MATTHEW 25:41) HOWEVER, THOSE WHO DO NOT MAKE THE CHOICE TO BELIEVE IN GOD WHILE THEY ARE HERE ON EARTH WILL GO TO HELL WHEN THEY DIE. "AND THESE WILL GO AWAY INTO ETERNAL PUNISHMENT, BUT THE RIGHTEOUS INTO ETERNAL LIFE". (MATTHEW 25: 46)

MANKIND CAN CHOOSE ONLY WHILE THEY ARE HERE ON THIS EARTH WHETHER THEY WANT TO GO TO HEAVEN OR TO HELL. ONCE THEY DIE, THEY NO LONGER HAVE A CHOICE.

THAT IS THE MOST IMPORTANT DECISION YOU WILL EVER MAKE!

REMEMBER WHAT WE LEARNED IN THE INTRODUCTION? A PERSON NEVER REALLY DIES. HIS LIFE GOES SOMEWHERE ELSE. ONCE A LIFE IS CONCEIVED, WHETHER IT IS IN THE FIRST MOMENTS AFTER CONCEPTION OR WHETHER IT IS AT THE TIME OF DEATH, IT NEVER DIES. GOD CREATED LIFE. ANYTHING GIVEN LIFE CANNOT JUST CEASE TO EXIST. LIFE IS ETERNAL. OUR SOULS AND SPIRITS WILL LIVE ETERNALLY, EITHER IN HEAVEN OR HELL.

WE MUST STUDY WHAT THE BIBLE SAYS ABOUT HELL. WE FIND THE ACCOUNT OF WHAT HELL IS LIKE IN LUKE 16:19-31.

"NOW THERE WAS A CERTAIN RICH MAN, AND HE HABITUALLY DRESSED IN PURPLE AND FINE LINEN, GAILY LIVING IN SPLENDOR EVERY DAY.

"AND A CERTAIN POOR MAN NAMED LAZARUS WAS LAID AT HIS GATE, COVERED WITH SORES, AND LONGING TO BE FED WITH CRUMBS WHICH WERE FALLING FROM THE RICH MAN'S TABLE; BESIDES, EVEN THE DOGS WERE COMING AND LICKING HIS SORES.

"NOW IT CAME ABOUT THAT THE POOR MAN DIED AND HE WAS CARRIED AWAY BY THE ANGELS TO ABRAHAM'S BOSOM; AND THE RICH MAN ALSO DIED AND WAS BURIED.

"AND IN HADES (HELL) HE LIFTED UP HIS EYES, BEING IN TORMENT AND SAW ABRAHAM FAR AWAY AND LAZARUS IN HIS BOSOM. AND HE CRIED OUT AND SAID, "FATHER ABRAHAM, HAVE MERCY ON ME, AND SEND LAZARUS, THAT HE MAY DIP THE TIP OF HIS FINGER IN WATER AND COOL OFF MY TONGUE; FOR I AM IN AGONY IN THIS FLAME.

"BUT ABRAHAM SAID, 'CHILD, REMEMBER THAT DURING YOUR LIFE YOU RECEIVED YOUR GOOD THINGS, AND LIKEWISE LAZARUS BAD

THINGS, BUT NOW HE IS BEING COMFORTED HERE, AND YOU ARE IN AGONY.

'AND BESIDES ALL THIS, BETWEEN US AND YOU THERE IS A GREAT CHASM FIXED, IN ORDER THAT THOSE WHO WISH TO COME OVER FROM HERE TO YOU MAY NOT BE ABLE, AND THAT NONE MAY CROSS OVER FROM THERE TO US.'

"AND HE SAID, 'THEN I BEG YOU, FATHER, THAT YOU SEND HIM TO MY FATHER'S HOUSE FOR I HAVE FIVE BROTHERS THAT HE MAY WARN THEM, LEST THEY ALSO COME TO THIS PLACE OF TORMENT.'

"BUT ABRAHAM SAID, 'THEY HAVE MOSES AND THE PROPHETS; LET THEM HEAR THEM.'

"BUT HE SAID, 'NO, FATHER ABRAHAM, BUT IF SOMEONE GOES TO THEM FROM THE DEAD, THEY WILL REPENT!'

"BUT HE SAID TO HIM, 'IF THEY DO NOT LISTEN TO MOSES AND THE PROPHETS, NEITHER WILL THEY BE PERSUADED IF SOMEONE RISES FROM THE DEAD."

NOW LET US LOOK AT SOME KEY VERSES THAT EXPLAIN WHAT HELL IS REALLY LIKE, AND IN DOING THIS LET US REMEMBER THAT GOD IS A LOVING GOD. HE SENT HIS SON TO

DIE FOR EVERY PERSON ON THIS EARTH SO WE WOULD NOT HAVE TO GO TO HELL.

GOING TO HEAVEN OR HELL IS NOT A MATTER OF BEING RICH OR POOR. WHAT MATTERS TO GOD IS WHETHER WE ACCEPT THE SACRIFICE OF HIS SON, JESUS, AND THE FORGIVENESS OF SIN, ALLOWING HIM TO BE THE GOD OF OUR LIFE.

LUKE 16:23 SHOWS THAT HELL IS A PLACE OF TORMENT. SINCE WE GO THERE ETERNALLY, IF WE DO NOT CHOOSE GOD, WE WILL BE TORMENTED ETERNALLY.

LUKE 16:24 SHOWS US THAT HELL IS HOT AND IS AFLAME; IT IS ON FIRE AND THERE IS NO WATER THERE.

LUKE 16:26 SHOWS US THAT THERE IS A GREAT CHASM OR EXPANSE BETWEEN HEAVEN AND HELL; THIS CONFIRMS THE FACT THAT ONCE WE GO THERE, WE CANNOT CROSS OVER TO THE OTHER SIDE. WE STAY THERE!

NOW NOTICE THAT IN THESE VERSES THIS PERSON HAD EYES TO SEE. HE COULD HEAR WHAT ABRAHAM SAID TO HIM. HE COULD FEEL THE FIRE AND THE HEAT, BUT DID NOT BURN UP. HE WANTED WATER TO COOL THE TIP OF HIS TONGUE. HE BEGGED ABRAHAM TO SEND SOMEONE BACK TO HIS FATHER'S HOUSE TO WARN THEM ABOUT HELL AND TO

PERSUADE THEM TO CHOOSE GOD AND NOT
COME THERE. HE HAD A MEMORY.

JUST THINK OF IT. **THOSE WHO GO TO
HELL WILL LIVE ETERNALLY WITH THE
MEMORY OF THE CHOICE THEY COULD
HAVE MADE WHILE ON THE EARTH.** THAT
IS PERHAPS THE WORST PART OF BEING IN
HELL: KNOWING THAT ALL YOU HAD TO DO
WAS TO ACCEPT JESUS WHILE ON THE EARTH,
AND YOU WOULD HAVE GONE TO HEAVEN
INSTEAD.

"THE LORD IS NOT SLOW ABOUT HIS
PROMISE, AS SOME COUNT SLOWNESS, BUT
IS PATIENT TOWARD YOU, NOT WISHING FOR
ANY TO PERISH BUT FOR ALL TO COME TO
REPENTANCE." (II PETER 3:9)

LET US ALSO MAKE NOTE HERE ABRAHAM
TOLD HIM THAT THE PEOPLE ON EARTH HAD
MOSES AND THE PROPHETS. MOSES HAD THE
TEN COMMANDMENTS AND THE PROPHETS
HEARD FROM GOD AND TOLD MEN WHAT
HE REQUIRED OF THEM. IN OUR DAY, THAT
WOULD BE SYMBOLIC OF THE BIBLE AND MEN
AND WOMEN WHO WALK CLOSE TO GOD AND
HEAR FROM HIM TODAY.

THERE IS A HEAVEN. HEAVEN IS WHERE
THE CREATOR OF THE UNIVERSE LIVES AND
REIGNS. IN HEAVEN IS ALL THE LOVE, PEACE,
JOY AND FULFILLMENT THAT MAN HAS

LONGED FOR SINCE HE WAS BORN. THERE IS NO SIN, SICKNESS, TORMENT OR LACK THERE.

IN REVELATION 4:1-6 WE SEE A GLIMPSE OF WHAT HEAVEN IS LIKE:

"AFTER THESE THINGS I LOOKED, AND BEHOLD A DOOR STANDING OPEN IN HEAVEN, AND THE FIRST VOICE WHICH I HAD HEARD, LIKE THE SOUND OF A TRUMPET SPEAKING WITH ME, SAID, 'COME UP HERE, AND I WILL SHOW YOU WHAT MUST TAKE PLACE AFTER THESE THINGS.'

"IMMEDIATELY I WAS IN THE SPIRIT; AND BEHOLD, A THRONE WAS STANDING IN HEAVEN, AND ONE SITTING ON THE THRONE. "AND HE WHO WAS SITTING WAS LIKE A JASPER STONE AND A SARDIUS IN APPEARANCE; AND THERE WAS A RAINBOW AROUND THE THRONE, LIKE AN EMERALD IN APPEARANCE.

"AND AROUND THE THRONE WERE TWENTY-FOUR THRONES, AND UPON THE THRONES I SAW TWENTY-FOUR ELDERS SITTING, CLOTHED IN WHITE GARMENTS, AND GOLDEN CROWNS ON THEIR HEADS.

"AND FROM THE THRONE PROCEED FLASHES OF LIGHTNING AND SOUNDS AND PEALS OF THUNDER. AND THERE WERE SEVEN LAMPS OF FIRE BURNING BEFORE THE

THRONE, WHICH ARE THE SEVEN SPIRITS OF GOD;

"AND BEFORE THE THRONE THERE WAS A SEA OF GLASS LIKE CRYSTAL; AND IN THE CENTER AND AROUND THE THRONE, FOUR LIVING CREATURES FULL OF EYES IN FRONT AND BEHIND."

THEN IN REVELATION 21:3-8. WE READ ABOUT THE DESTINY OF EVERY PERSON WHO IS EVER BORN ON THIS EARTH IF THEY ACCEPT JESUS AS THEIR SAVIOR:

"AND I HEARD A LOUD VOICE FROM THE THRONE SAYING, 'BEHOLD, THE TABERNACLE OF GOD IS AMONG MEN, AND HE SHALL DWELL AMONG THEM, AND THEY SHALL BE HIS PEOPLE, AND GOD HIMSELF SHALL BE AMONG THEM,

'AND HE SHALL WIPE AWAY EVERY TEAR FROM THEIR EYES; AND THERE SHALL NO LONGER BE ANY DEATH; THERE SHALL NO LONGER BE ANY MOURNING, OR CRYING OR PAIN. THE FIRST THINGS HAVE PASSED AWAY.'

"AND HE WHO SITS ON THE THRONE SAID, 'BEHOLD, I AM MAKING ALL THINGS NEW.' AND HE SAID, 'WRITE, FOR THESE WORDS ARE FAITHFUL AND TRUE.'

"AND HE SAID TO ME, 'IT IS DONE. I AM THE ALPHA AND THE OMEGA, THE BEGINNING AND THE END. I WILL GIVE TO THE ONE WHO THIRSTS FROM THE SPRING OF THE WATER OF LIFE WITHOUT COST.

'HE WHO OVERCOMES SHALL INHERIT THESE THINGS, AND I WILL BE HIS GOD AND HE WILL BE MY SON.

'BUT FOR THE COWARDLY AND UNBELIEVING AND ABOMINABLE AND MURDERERS AND IMMORAL PERSONS AND SORCERERS AND IDOLATERS AND ALL LIARS, THEIR PART WILL BE IN THE LAKE THAT BURNS WITH FIRE AND BRIMSTONE, WHICH IS THE SECOND DEATH."

THE CHOICE IS OURS. WHILE WE ARE ON THIS EARTH WE MUST MAKE THE CHOICE TO ACCEPT JESUS AS OUR LORD AND SAVIOR AND LIVE ETERNALLY IN HEAVEN, OR REJECT WHAT HE DID FOR US AND LIVE ETERNALLY IN HELL.

HEAVEN IS A WONDERFUL PLACE. IT IS FAR BEYOND ANYTHING WE CAN COMPREHEND. IT IS COMPLETE AND THRIVES ON THE LOVE, PEACE AND JOY OF GOD.

WHAT IS EVEN MORE WONDERFUL, WE CAN HAVE THAT LOVE, PEACE AND JOY HERE ON EARTH WHILE WE ARE WAITING TO GO

TO HEAVEN. ONCE WE ACCEPT JESUS AS OUR LORD AND SAVIOR, EVEN THOUGH WE GO THROUGH TROUBLES HERE ON EARTH DUE TO SATAN AND THE SIN HERE, WE HAVE THE LOVE AND PROTECTION OF OUR GOD TO SEE US THROUGH. WE HAVE LOVE, JOY, PEACE, PROTECTION AND FULFILLMENT WHEN WE MAKE HIM OUR LORD.

GOD WILL MAKE THE WAY WHERE THERE IS NO WAY. HE PROTECTS US. HE PROSPERS US AND ANSWERS OUR PRAYERS AND DAILY NEEDS. HE IS TRULY A GOD OF LOVE. HE IS TRULY A FATHER WHO CARES, EVEN WHEN OUR OWN FATHERS DON'T. HE OPENS HIS WORD TO OUR MINDS AND SHOWS US HOW TO LIVE ABOVE THE CIRCUMSTANCES THAT COME AGAINST US. IT IS HIS GOOD PLEASURE TO SHOW US THE MIRACULOUS POWER HE HAS ON BEHALF OF THOSE WHO CHOOSE TO ACCEPT AND SERVE HIM.

WHAT IS EVEN MORE IMPORTANT, WE NO LONGER BELONG TO SATAN, THE GOD OF THIS WORLD. WE BECOME THE PROPERTY OF THE GOD WHO CREATED US ONCE AGAIN. "FOR HE DELIVERED US FROM THE DOMAIN OF DARKNESS, AND TRANSFERRED US INTO THE KINGDOM OF HIS BELOVED SON, IN WHOM WE HAVE REDEMPTION, THE FORGIVENESS OF SINS." (COLOSSIANS 1:13—14)

HE CAN CHANGE CIRCUMSTANCES. HE CAN HEAL SICK AND DISEASED MINDS AND BODIES. HE CAN HEAL OUR RELATIONSHIPS AND MARRIAGES. HE CAN CAUSE US TO PROSPER. HE PROTECTS US AND LOVES US WITH A PERFECT LOVE, A LOVE WE CAN NEVER KNOW UNLESS WE CHOOSE TO RECEIVE HIM AS OUR LORD AND SAVIOR.

TELL HIM NOW, THIS MINUTE, THAT YOU WANT TO KNOW HIM. ASK HIM TO BE YOUR LORD. ASK HIM TO OPEN YOUR MIND TO HIS WORD AND TO SHOW YOU TRUTH. HE IS WATCHING YOU RIGHT NOW. HE IS WAITING FOR YOU TO ASK HIM, SO HE CAN SHOW YOU HOW MUCH HE LOVES YOU.

IF YOU ASK, YOU WILL FEEL HIS PRESENCE. YOU WILL FEEL HIS PEACE AND LOVE. HE LOVES YOU SO MUCH, HE SENT HIS SON, JESUS TO DIE FOR YOU SO YOU COULD BE HIS CHILD FROM THIS MOMENT ON.

ASK HIM NOW, BEFORE YOU GO ANY FURTHER. THEN YOU WILL BE ABLE TO BETTER UNDERSTAND WHAT THE REST OF THIS BOOK IS ALL ABOUT. YOU DON'T HAVE TO UNDERSTAND IT AT THIS POINT. ALL YOU HAVE TO DO IS ASK AND EXPERIENCE HIS LOVING PRESENCE.

HE WILL THEN OPEN YOUR SPIRITUAL MIND TO UNDERSTAND WHAT HIS WORD SAYS IN THE BIBLE AND IN THIS BOOK.

HOW DID GOD REDEEM MAN?

IT IS NECESSARY FOR US TO SEE THAT MAN, AFTER THE FALL, WAS TOTALLY SEPARATED FROM GOD. HE HAD FORFEITED EVERY RIGHT WHICH GOD HAD BESTOWED ON HIM. HE HAD COMMITTED <u>TREASON</u> IN THE EYES OF GOD. HE NO LONGER HAD ANY HOPE, AND WAS UNDER THE POWER OF SATAN WHERE EVIL AND DEATH REIGNED.

EVEN MORE, HE HAD THE SIN NATURE OF SATAN. HE WAS IN UNION WITH SATAN'S NATURE, SPIRITUALLY DEAD, A CHILD OF SATAN AND NO LONGER A CHILD OF GOD.

THIS IS THE SAME CONDITION MANKIND IS IN TODAY, UNTIL HE TURNS TO GOD FOR SALVATION FROM SATAN'S POWER.

MAN BECAME A LEGAL CHILD OF SATAN WHICH ALSO MADE HIM A LEGAL CRIMINAL IN THE SIGHT OF GOD. IF HE WERE EVER TO STAND RIGHT WITH GOD AGAIN, IT HAD

TO BE DONE ON LEGAL GROUNDS. GOD IS PERFECT AND HAS TO BE JUST.

GOD WAS AND STILL IS A GOD OF LOVE. HE STILL CARED WHAT HAPPENED TO MAN. HE SAW THAT MAN'S ONLY HOPE WAS FOR A MEDIATOR, SOMEONE WHO COULD RESTORE MAN BACK TO GOD AND LEGALLY DEFEAT SATAN, SOMEONE WHO COULD FULFILL THE PENALTIES OF DEATH AND HELL.

BUT, GOD HAD TO DO IT IN SUCH A WAY THAT MAN STILL HAD A CHOICE. **GOD WILL NOT OVERRIDE MAN'S WILL OR HIS RIGHT TO CHOOSE.**

THE ONLY WAY TO LEGALLY AND JUSTLY REDEEM MAN FROM THE POWER OF SATAN AND BACK INTO COMMUNION WITH GOD WAS TO PRODUCE A SINLESS MAN AS A SUBSTITUTE FOR FALLEN MAN.

THIS MAN WOULD HAVE TO LIVE A TOTALLY SINLESS LIFE ON EARTH, NOT ALLOWING SATAN TO TEMPT HIM IN ANY WAY. HE WOULD THEN HAVE TO FULFILL THE PENALTY FOR ALL MANKIND FOR THE SIN, SICKNESS, DISEASE AND TORMENT THAT SATAN PUT ON MAN BY TAKING IT ALL ON HIMSELF. HE WOULD ALSO HAVE TO GO TO HELL IN MAN'S PLACE TO FULFILL THE DEATH PENALTY THAT WAS REQUIRED.

ONCE ALL THESE REQUIREMENTS WERE FULFILLED, SATAN WOULD NO LONGER HAVE A LEGAL RIGHT TO KEEP MAN. THIS MAN WOULD THEN HAVE CONQUERED SATAN, DEATH AND HELL AND WOULD THEN RAISE FROM THE GRAVE AND GIVE THE EARTH BACK TO MAN TO CHOOSE ONCE AGAIN FOR HIMSELF WHETHER TO SERVE SATAN OR GOD.

IN ORDER TO CHOOSE THIS MAN, GOD COULDN'T CREATE ANOTHER MAN LIKE ADAM AND PLACE HIM ON THE EARTH. THE EARTH NO LONGER LEGALLY BELONGED TO GOD. HE HAD GIVEN IT TO ADAM, AND ADAM HAD GIVEN IT TO SATAN.

HE COULDN'T USE A MAN ALREADY ON THE EARTH TO PRODUCE A SINLESS SUBSTITUTE BECAUSE ALL MEN ON THE EARTH WERE DESCENDANTS OF ADAM, WITH THE SIN NATURE OF ADAM.

THERE WAS REALLY ONLY ONE WAY THAT GOD COULD REDEEM MAN. <u>GOD WOULD HAVE TO COME HIMSELF</u>. HE WOULD HAVE TO FULFILL THE PENALTIES OF MAN'S SIN, HIMSELF. <u>HE WOULD HAVE TO BE BOTH</u> GOD AND MAN IN ONE BODY.

THIS IS EXACTLY WHAT HE DID. WE HAVE THE ACCOUNT OF IT IN THE GOSPELS OF MATTHEW AND LUKE. THE MOST COMPLETE

ACCOUNT WE HAVE OF WHAT HAPPENED IS IN LUKE 1:26-38.

"NOW IN THE SIXTH MONTH THE ANGEL GABRIEL WAS SENT FROM GOD TO A CITY IN GALILEE, CALLED NAZARETH, TO A VIRGIN ENGAGED TO A MAN WHOSE NAME WAS JOSEPH, OF THE DESCENDANTS OF DAVID; AND THE VIRGIN'S NAME WAS MARY.

AND COMING IN, HE SAID TO HER, 'HAIL FAVORED ONE! THE LORD IS WITH YOU.' BUT SHE WAS GREATLY TROUBLED AT THIS STATEMENT, AND KEPT PONDERING WHAT KIND OF SALUTATION THIS MIGHT BE.

AND THE ANGEL SAID TO HER, 'DO NOT BE AFRAID, MARY; FOR YOU HAVE FOUND FAVOR WITH GOD. AND BEHOLD YOU WILL CONCEIVE IN YOUR WOMB, AND BEAR A SON, AND YOU SHALL NAME HIM JESUS.

HE WILL BE GREAT, AND WILL BE CALLED THE SON OF THE MOST HIGH; AND THE LORD GOD WILL GIVE HIM THE THRONE OF HIS FATHER DAVID; AND HE WILL REIGN OVER THE HOUSE OF JACOB FOREVER; AND HIS KINGDOM WILL HAVE NO END.'

AND MARY SAID TO THE ANGEL, 'HOW CAN THIS BE, SINCE I AM A VIRGIN?'

AND THE ANGEL ANSWERED AND SAID TO HER, 'THE HOLY SPIRIT WILL COME UPON YOU, AND THE POWER OF THE MOST HIGH WILL OVERSHADOW YOU, AND FOR THAT REASON THE HOLY OFFSPRING SHALL BE CALLED THE SON OF GOD.

AND BEHOLD, EVEN YOUR RELATIVE ELIZABETH HAS ALSO CONCEIVED A SON IN HER OLD AGE; AND SHE WHO WAS CALLED BARREN IS NOW IN HER SIXTH MONTH.

FOR NOTHING SHALL BE IMPOSSIBLE WITH GOD!'

AND MARY SAID, 'BEHOLD, THE SERVANT OF THE LORD; BE IT DONE TO ME ACCORDING TO YOUR WORD.' AND THE ANGEL DEPARTED FROM HER."

WE KNOW THAT THE EGG THAT THE WOMAN PRODUCES HAS NO LIFE IN IT UNTIL IT IS FERTILIZED. SO, IN ORDER FOR A CHILD TO BE BORN WITHOUT THE SIN NATURE, THIS EGG MUST BE CONCEIVED BY GOD, HIMSELF.

WE MUST ALSO REALIZE THAT THE ONLY WAY THAT GOD COULD COME TO EARTH AND LEGALLY LIVE HERE TO OVERCOME SATAN WAS TO COME IN THE FORM OF A MAN AND TO BE TEMPTED BY SATAN JUST LIKE OTHER MEN. **HE HAD TO OVERCOME SIN BY NOT SINNING IN ANY WAY**.

"SINCE THEN WE HAVE A GREAT HIGH PRIEST WHO HAS PASSED THROUGH THE HEAVENS, JESUS THE SON OF GOD, LET US HOLD FAST OUR CONFESSION. "FOR WE DO NOT HAVE A HIGH PRIEST WHO CANNOT SYMPATHIZE WITH OUR WEAKNESSES, BUT ONE WHO HAS BEEN TEMPTED IN ALL THINGS AS WE ARE, YET WITHOUT SIN." (HEBREWS 4:14-15)

GOD DID COME TO EARTH, AND HE CAME IN THE FORM OF A MAN. <u>HE WAS BOTH THE SON OF MAN AND THE SON OF GOD</u>. "FOR GOD SO LOVED THE WORLD THAT HE GAVE HIS ONLY BEGOTTEN SON, THAT WHOEVER BELIEVES IN HIM SHALL NOT PERISH BUT HAVE ETERNAL LIFE. FOR GOD DID NOT SEND HIS SON INTO THE WORLD IN ORDER TO CONDEMN THE WORLD, BUT THAT THE WORLD MIGHT BE SAVED THROUGH HIM." (JOHN 3:16 -17)

OUR FATHER, GOD, SENT HIS SON TO US. HIS NAME IS JESUS. JESUS LIVED A SINLESS LIFE HERE ON EARTH, DOING MANY MIRACLES ALONG THE WAY. HE SHOWED US HOW TO LIVE ABOVE SIN, DISEASE AND DEATH. HE OVERCAME IT ALL FOR US.

HE THEN SUFFERED WITH ALL THE SIN, PAIN AND SCORN THAT WAS RIGHTFULLY DUE US, BY DYING ON A CROSS. HE TOOK IT

ALL FOR US, SO THAT WE WOULDN'T HAVE TO.

THEN HE WENT DOWN INTO HELL AND WAS THERE THREE DAYS AND THREE NIGHTS SUFFERING THE TERRIBLE TORMENT THAT SHOULD BE OURS, SO THAT WE COULD HAVE THE RIGHT TO CHOOSE NOT TO GO THERE. "FOR JUST AS JONAH WAS THREE DAYS AND THREE NIGHTS IN THE BELLY OF THE SEA MONSTER, SO SHALL THE SON OF MAN BE THREE DAYS AND THREE NIGHTS IN THE HEART (BELLY) OF THE EARTH." (MATTHEW 12:40) (THIS SHOWS US WHERE HELL IS. IT IS IN THE CENTER OF THE EARTH. HASN'T SCIENCE PROVEN THAT THE CENTER OF THE EARTH IS AFLAME WITH FIRE?)

THEN HE AROSE FROM HELL THE CONQUEROR OF SIN, SICKNESS, DEATH AND ALL OF THE TORMENT THAT SATAN COULD PUT ON US.

"NOW AFTER THE SABBATH, AS IT BEGAN TO DAWN TOWARD THE FIRST DAY OF THE WEEK, MARY MAGDALENE AND THE OTHER MARY CAME TO LOOK AT THE GRAVE.

"AND BEHOLD, A SEVERE EARTHQUAKE OCCURRED, FOR AN ANGEL OF THE LORD DESCENDED FROM HEAVEN AND CAME AND ROLLED AWAY THE STONE AND SAT UPON IT. AND HIS APPEARANCE WAS LIKE LIGHTNING,

AND HIS GARMENT AS WHITE AS SNOW; AND THE GUARDS SHOOK FOR FEAR OF HIM, AND BECAME LIKE DEAD MEN.

"AND THE ANGEL ANSWERED AND SAID TO THE WOMEN, 'DO NOT BE AFRAID; FOR I KNOW THAT YOU ARE LOOKING FOR JESUS WHO HAS BEEN CRUCIFIED.

'HE IS NOT HERE, FOR HE HAS RISEN, JUST AS HE SAID. COME AND SEE THE PLACE WHERE HE WAS LYING. AND GO QUICKLY AND TELL HIS DISCIPLES THAT HE HAS RISEN FROM THE DEAD; AND BEHOLD, HE IS GOING BEFORE YOU INTO GALILEE, THERE YOU WILL SEE HIM; BEHOLD, I HAVE TOLD YOU.'" (MATTHEW 28:1-7)

JESUS ROSE FROM THE DEAD, THE CONQUEROR OF SATAN AND DEATH. "- -AND I WAS DEAD, AND BEHOLD I AM ALIVE FOREVERMORE, AND I HAVE THE KEYS OF DEATH AND OF HADES (HELL.)" (REVELATION 1:18) "AND HE (JESUS) IS THE BEGINNING, THE FIRST-BORN FROM THE DEAD; SO THAT HE HIMSELF MIGHT COME TO HAVE FIRST PLACE IN EVERYTHING." (COLOSSIANS 1:18)

HE IS NOW THE SAVIOR OF ALL MANKIND. ALL WE HAVE TO DO IS TURN TO HIM, AND ASK HIM TO BE OUR LORD.

GOD DOES LOVE US. HE CARES VERY MUCH WHAT HAPPENS TO YOU.

THE BIBLE SAYS, "GOD IS NOT WISHING FOR ANY TO PERISH, BUT FOR ALL TO COME TO REPENTANCE. (II PETER 3:9)

WE CAN NOW BECOME CHILDREN OF GOD LIKE ADAM WAS WHEN GOD CREATED HIM. WE CAN COMMUNE WITH OUR FATHER, GOD. WE CAN BE IN RIGHT-STANDING WITH HIM, WITH ALL THE PRIVILEGES THAT ADAM ONCE HAD. IT SEEMS IMPOSSIBLE TO OUR MINDS; BUT WE WILL STUDY THE SCRIPTURES TO SEE JUST WHAT JESUS DID AND WHAT WE HAVE TO DO TO WALK WITH HIM.

JESUS WAS RAISED A BORN AGAIN, NEW CREATION. WE CAN NOW BE BORN AGAIN, HERE ON EARTH. TO BE BORN AGAIN MEANS THAT OUR SPIRIT, ONCE WE ACCEPT JESUS AS OUR LORD AND SAVIOR, IS BORN FROM A DEAD SPIRIT TO A NEW ETERNAL SPIRIT, ALIVE TO GOD AND DEAD TO SIN AND SATAN.

WE CANNOT EVEN IMAGINE WHAT GOD HAS IN STORE FOR US ONCE WE ACCEPT HIM.

"THINGS WHICH EYE HAS NOT SEEN AND EAR HAS NOT HEARD, AND WHICH HAVE NOT ENTERED THE HEART OF MAN, ALL THAT GOD HAS PREPARED FOR THOSE WHO LOVE HIM." (I CORINTHIANS 2:9)

HOW ARE WE BORN AGAIN?

IT IS REALLY VERY EASY TO BECOME BORN AGAIN. WE MUST GO TO GOD'S WORD TO FIND THE WAY OF SALVATION.

IN MATTHEW 7:14 WE READ, "THE WAY IS NARROW THAT LEADS TO LIFE, AND FEW ARE THOSE WHO FIND IT." IN COMPARISON WITH THE NUMBER OF PEOPLE WHO ARE ON THIS EARTH, THERE ARE FEW WHO REALLY FIND THE TRUTH AND THEREBY RECEIVE ETERNAL LIFE FROM GOD.

GOING BACK TO JOHN 3: 1-5 AGAIN, REMEMBER NICODEMUS, THE PHARISEE WHO CAME TO JESUS AND WANTED TO KNOW HOW TO BE BORN AGAIN? IN JOHN 3:3 JESUS STATES "UNLESS ONE IS BORN AGAIN, HE CANNOT SEE (OR UNDERSTAND) THE KINGDOM OF GOD." IN VERSE 5 HE STATES THAT "UNLESS ONE IS BORN OF THE WATER AND THE SPIRIT, HE CANNOT ENTER INTO THE KINGDOM OF GOD."

THE ONLY WAY NICODEMUS EVER KNEW THAT A PERSON COULD BE BORN WAS BY NATURAL BIRTH. THAT IS THE ONLY WAY WE KNOW TOO. UNTIL NOW, WE HAVEN' T KNOWN THAT WE WERE SPIRITUALLY DEAD AND THAT OUR SPIRITS COULD BE BORN AGAIN.

IN ORDER TO SEE WHAT JESUS IS TALKING ABOUT, LET US LOOK AT A NATURAL BIRTH AS A MEANS OF COMPARISON.

BEFORE A BABY IS BORN, IT IS IN DARKNESS INSIDE ITS MOTHER'S WOMB. IT MUST BE BORN IN ORDER TO SEE LIGHT. II CORINTHIANS 4:4 STATES . . . "THE GOD OF THIS WORLD HAS BLINDED THE MINDS OF THE UNBELIEVING, THAT THEY MIGHT NOT SEE THE LIGHT OF THE GOSPEL OF THE GLORY OF CHRIST."

UNTIL WE ARE BORN AGAIN, WE ARE IN SPIRITUAL DARKNESS, LED BY SATAN, THE GOD OF THIS WORLD. FOR "WE KNOW THAT NO ONE WHO IS BORN OF GOD SINS; BUT HE WHO WAS BORN OF GOD KEEPS HIM AND THE EVIL ONE DOES NOT TOUCH HIM. WE KNOW THAT WE ARE OF GOD, AND THE WHOLE WORLD LIES IN THE POWER OF THE EVIL ONE." (I JOHN 5:18-19)

WE MUST BE BORN OF GOD . . . BORN AGAIN . . . BEFORE WE CAN SEE THE LIGHT OR UNDERSTAND GOD'S WORD. WE ARE IN

SPIRITUAL DARKNESS LIKE AN UNBORN BABY UNTIL WE ARE BORN AGAIN. WE CANNOT SEE THE KINGDOM OF GOD. THAT IS WHAT GOD'S WORD SAYS.

WE KNOW NOTHING OF GOD'S WORLD OR HIS WAYS OR REQUIREMENTS. WE ARE BLINDED AND CANNOT SEE THE GLORIOUS LIGHT OF THE GOSPEL OF GOD ANY MORE THAN AN UNBORN BABY CAN SEE THE LIGHT OF THE WORLD IN WHICH IT WILL LIVE UNTIL IT IS BORN.

BUT...HOW ARE WE TO BECOME "BORN AGAIN' AND ENTER THE KINGDOM OF GOD?

ACCORDING TO ROMANS 10:9-11, "IF YOU CONFESS WITH YOUR MOUTH JESUS AS LORD, AND BELIEVE IN YOUR HEART THAT GOD RAISED HIM FROM THE DEAD, YOU SHALL BE SAVED. FOR WITH THE HEART MAN BELIEVES, RESULTING IN RIGHTEOUSNESS AND WITH THE MOUTH HE CONFESSES, RESULTING IN SALVATION. FOR THE SCRIPTURE SAYS, 'WHOEVER BELIEVES IN HIM WILL NOT BE DISAPPOINTED.'"

SO, FIRST WE MUST BELIEVE IN WHAT GOD DID FOR US THROUGH HIS SON, JESUS. WE MUST NOT ONLY BELIEVE IT IN OUR HEART, BUT WE MUST CONFESS IT WITH OUR MOUTH.

ONCE WE HAVE DONE THIS JOHN 3:5 STATES VERY CLEARLY, "...UNLESS ONE IS BORN OF THE WATER AND THE SPIRIT, HE CANNOT ENTER INTO THE KINGDOM OF GOD." SO ACCORDING TO HIS WORD, WE MUST BE BORN OF <u>WATER</u> AND THE <u>SPIRIT</u> IN ORDER TO ENTER INTO THE KINGDOM OF GOD.

WHEN A BABY IS BORN, THE WATER BREAKS FORTH AND CLEANSES THE WAY FOR THE BABY TO PASS INTO IT'S NEW LIFE OUTSIDE OF THE DARKNESS OF THE MOTHER'S WOMB. IT THEN COMES THROUGH THAT STRAIGHT AND NARROW PASSAGE INTO THE WORLD. THAT IS THE WAY WE ARE TO BE BORN AGAIN. WE MUST SEARCH THE WORD OF GOD FOR HIS WAY, WHICH IS STRAIGHT AND NARROW. (MATTHEW 7:14)

ACTS 2:38 GIVES US OUR ANSWER. PETER EXPLAINS THAT THE WAY GOD REQUIRES US TO ENTER HIS KINGDOM IS TO "REPENT, EVERY ONE OF YOU, AND BE BAPTIZED IN THE NAME OF JESUS CHRIST FOR THE FORGIVENESS OF YOUR SINS, AND YOU SHALL RECEIVE THE GIFT OF THE HOLY SPIRIT."

SO WE SEE THERE ARE TWO THINGS THAT GOD REQUIRES OF US IN ORDER TO BE BORN AGAIN. FIRST WE MUST REPENT AND ASK GOD TO FORGIVE US OF OUR SINS. ONCE WE HAVE DONE THIS, WE ARE FORGIVEN AND CLEANSED FROM ALL UNRIGHTEOUSNESS

AND WE BECOME CHILDREN OF GOD OUR CREATOR. (I JOHN 1:9) SECOND, WE ARE TO BE BAPTIZED IN THE NAME OF JESUS CHRIST. WHEN WE DO THIS HE PROMISES TO GIVE US THE GIFT OF THE HOLY SPIRIT. FIRST WE MUST DO OUR PART. THEN HE WILL DO HIS PART.

HOW DOES MAN REPENT?

WE ARE DEAD IN OUR SINS BEFORE WE ARE BORN AGAIN. JESUS TOOK OUR PLACE AND DIED FOR OUR SIN WHICH OPENED THE WAY FOR US TO BE FORGIVEN AND HAVE DOMINION OVER THIS EARTH ONCE AGAIN.

GOD REQUIRES OBEDIENCE TO HIS WORD AND NOT OBEDIENCE TO THE WORDS AND TRADITIONS OF MEN. WE NOW KNOW THAT GOD REVEALS THE MYSTERIES OF HIS WORD TO THOSE WHO TURN TO HIM. SO WE NEED TO LOOK INTO HIS WORD FOR THE ANSWER TO THIS QUESTION, BECAUSE IT IS PERHAPS ONE OF THE MOST IMPORTANT QUESTIONS WE WILL EVER ASK.

ACCORDING TO ACTS 2:38, THE FIRST THING WE MUST DO IS TO REPENT FOR THE SINS WE HAVE COMMITTED. THE WORD "REPENT" MEANS TO FEEL SORRY TO THE POINT WHERE A PERSON CHANGES HIS OR HER MIND AND WAYS. ONCE THE MIND IS CHANGED, THE PERSON STOPS DOING THOSE THINGS THAT ARE NOT PLEASING TO GOD.

REPENTANCE IS NOT MERELY BEING SORRY FOR WHAT WE HAVE DONE. <u>IT IS A DECISION FROM THE HEART TO TURN AROUND AND GO IN THE OPPOSITE DIRECTION</u>. THIS IS A FREE ACT OF OUR WILL. GOD WILL NOT VIOLATE OUR WILL. IF WE CHOOSE TO DISBELIEVE HIS WORD AND TURN OUR BACK ON HIM, HE WILL ALLOW US TO DO SO. HOWEVER, IF WE CHOOSE TO REPENT, TURN AROUND AND LIVE FOR HIM, HE WILL GIVE US HIS POWER BY THE HOLY SPIRIT TO DO SO. **THE CHOICE IS OURS**!

OUR GOD IS A HOLY GOD. HE REQUIRES OBEDIENCE TO HIS WORD ONCE WE HAVE BEEN SHOWN THE TRUTH AND THE WAY TO GO. WE WILL NEVER FULLY UNDERSTAND WHAT THE KINGDOM OF GOD IS ALL ABOUT UNTIL WE ARE BORN AGAIN AND MAKE A COMMITMENT TO GOD AND TO HIS WORD. IT IS VERY IMPORTANT THAT WE DO AS HIS WORD SAYS TO THE BEST OF OUR ABILITY.

GOD DOES NOT DEMAND OUR OBEDIENCE AS A FATHER SITTING IN HEAVEN WITH A BIG STICK READY TO STRIKE US IF WE DON'T OBEY HIM. HOWEVER, HE HAS PUT PRINCIPLES IN HIS WORD FOR OUR OWN GOOD. HE CREATED US. HE KNOWS THE PROBLEMS WE HAVE HERE ON EARTH. HE CAME TO EARTH IN THE BODY OF JESUS AND THE BIBLE SAYS HE SUFFERED EVERYTHING WE SUFFER, BUT HE NEVER GAVE IN TO SIN. EVERYTHING HE REQUIRES

OF US IS TO SAVE US. HE CREATED US AND HE KNOWS WHAT WILL HARM US AND WHAT WILL SAVE US.

SO, ONCE WE HAVE DECIDED TO FOLLOW GOD, WE MUST ASK HIM TO FORGIVE US FOR THE PAST SINS WE HAVE COMMITTED. IT IS JUST THAT SIMPLE. HE IS A GOD OF LOVE AND FORGIVENESS. HE CAME TO EARTH AND TOOK THE PUNISHMENT FOR THE SINS OF THE WHOLE WORLD FOR ALL TIME. SO WE COULD BE SET FREE.

LET'S LOOK AT SOME SCRIPTURES TO CONFIRM THESE STATEMENTS:

"FOR GOD SO LOVED THE WORLD THAT HE GAVE HIS ONLY BEGOTTEN SON, THAT WHOEVER BELIEVES IN HIM SHOULD NOT PERISH, BUT HAVE ETERNAL LIFE. FOR GOD DID NOT SEND THE SON INTO THE WORLD TO JUDGE THE WORLD, BUT THAT THE WORLD SHOULD BE SAVED THROUGH HIM." (JOHN 3: 16-17)

"THUS IT IS WRITTEN, THAT CHRIST SHOULD SUFFER AND RISE FROM THE DEAD THE THIRD DAY; AND THAT REPENTANCE FOR FORGIVENESS OF SINS SHOULD BE PROCLAIMED IN HIS NAME TO ALL THE NATIONS, BEGINNING FROM JERUSALEM." (LUKE 24:46-47)

"FOR HE DELIVERED US FROM THE DOMAIN OF DARKNESS AND TRANSFERRED US TO THE KINGDOM OF HIS BELOVED SON, IN WHOM WE HAVE REDEMPTION AND THE FORGIVENESS OF SINS." (COLOSSIANS 1:13-14)

"IF WE CONFESS OUR SINS, HE IS FAITHFUL AND RIGHTEOUS TO FORGIVE US OUR SINS AND TO CLEANSE US FROM ALL UNRIGHTEOUSNESS. (I JOHN 1:9)

"...AND IF ANYONE SINS, WE HAVE AN ADVOCATE WITH THE FATHER, JESUS CHRIST, THE RIGHTEOUS: AND HE HIMSELF IS THE PROPITIATION (SUBSTITUTE) FOR OUR SINS; AND NOT FOR OURS ONLY, BUT ALSO FOR THE SINS OF THE WHOLE WORLD."(I JOHN 2:1-2)

SO, WE SEE THAT WE CAN COME TO OUR FATHER GOD, ASK HIS FORGIVENESS AND HE IS FAITHFUL TO FORGIVE US AND TO CLEANSE US FROM ALL UNRIGHTEOUSNESS. WHEN WE DO THAT, HE RECEIVES US AND THE DOOR IS OPEN TO BE BORN AGAIN.

THAT BRINGS US TO THE NEXT STEP IN OUR QUEST TO ENTER INTO GOD'S KINGDOM AND RECEIVE ETERNAL LIFE IN HEAVEN WITH HIM. THE NEXT PART OF ACTS 2:38 TELLS US: "LET EACH OF YOU BE BAPTIZED IN THE NAME OF JESUS CHRIST FOR THE FORGIVENESS OF YOUR SINS."

HOW IS MAN BORN OF THE WATER?

WE ARE BORN OF THE WATER THROUGH BAPTISM IN WATER. IN ACTS 2:38, GOD GAVE US SPECIFIC INSTRUCTIONS TO BE WATER BAPTIZED. MANY BELIEVE THAT WATER BAPTISM IS NOT IMPORTANT. BUT WE HAVE TO BELIEVE WHAT GOD' S WORD SAYS...NOT WHAT PEOPLE BELIEVE.

THE HOLY SPIRIT SHOWS US THINGS IN GOD'S WORD AND THEN LAYS THEM ON OUR HEARTS TO FOLLOW THE WORD HE HAS SHOWN US. BEING WATER BAPTIZED IS SIMPLY AN ACT OF OBEDIENCE TO HIS WORD. IT IS SYMBOLIC OF HUMBLING OURSELVES BEFORE HIM. IT IS A STRIPPING AWAY OF ALL PRIDE AND AN ACT ON OUR PART TO SHOW HIM THAT WE REALLY DO WANT TO LIVE IN HIS KINGDOM, WITH HIM AS OUR LORD.

WHEN WE ARE BAPTIZED IN WATER, WE ARE SYMBOLICALLY FORGIVEN AND CLEANSED OF SIN. THE WAY IS PREPARED FOR

US TO COME INTO THE NEW LIFE GOD HAS FOR US.

LET'S READ IT IN ROMANS 6: 3-11. "OR DO YOU NOT KNOW THAT ALL OF US WHO HAVE BEEN BAPTIZED INTO CHRIST JESUS HAVE BEEN BAPTIZED INTO HIS DEATH? THEREFORE, WE HAVE BEEN BURIED WITH HIM THROUGH BAPTISM INTO DEATH IN ORDER THAT AS CHRIST WAS RAISED FROM THE DEAD THROUGH THE GLORY OF THE FATHER, SO WE TOO MIGHT WALK IN <u>NEWNESS OF LIFE</u>.

"FOR IF WE HAVE BECOME UNITED WITH HIM IN THE LIKENESS OF HIS DEATH, CERTAINLY WE SHALL BE ALSO IN THE LIKENESS OF HIS RESURRECTION. KNOWING THIS, <u>THAT OUR OLD SELF WAS CRUCIFIED WITH HIM</u>, THAT OUR BODY OF SIN MIGHT BE DONE AWAY WITH, THAT WE SHOULD NO LONGER BE SLAVES TO SIN; <u>FOR HE WHO HAS DIED IS FREED FROM SIN</u>.

"NOW IF WE HAVE DIED WITH CHRIST, WE BELIEVE THAT WE SHALL ALSO LIVE WITH HIM, KNOWING THAT CHRIST HAVING BEEN RAISED FROM THE DEAD IS NEVER TO DIE AGAIN; DEATH NO LONGER IS MASTER OVER HIM. <u>FOR THE DEATH THAT HE DIED, HE DIED TO SIN, **ONCE FOR ALL**</u>; BUT THE LIFE THAT HE LIVES, HE LIVES TO GOD. EVEN SO CONSIDER YOURSELVES TO BE DEAD TO SIN BUT ALIVE TO GOD IN CHRIST JESUS."

ONCE WE ARE BAPTIZED ACCORDING TO HIS WORD, WE ARE SYMBOLICALLY RAISED FROM THE DEAD (BORN AGAIN) SO THAT WE MIGHT WALK IN NEWNESS OF LIFE. IT IS THE NARROW WAY. NOT TOO MANY WILL CHOOSE TO WALK IT. BUT OH THE JOY OF FOLLOWING HIM IN THE WATERS OF BAPTISM! THERE IS NOTHING LIKE IT ON EARTH.

WHEN WE GO DOWN UNDER THE WATER IN BAPTISM, WE USUALLY DO NOT FEEL ANYTHING. BUT WHEN WE COME UP OUT OF THE WATER, WE FEEL CLEAN INSIDE. WE CAN FEEL HIS PRESENCE. IT IS A MIRACULOUS FEELING. THERE IS NO OTHER FEELING LIKE IT; AND ONLY WHEN WE DO IT, CAN WE REALLY EXPERIENCE IT.

WE ARE ALIVE FROM THE DEAD WHEN WE ARE BORN AGAIN ACCORDING TO ROMANS 6:13. JUST AS A NEWBORN BABY COMES INTO THE WORLD A NEW LITTLE CREATION, SO ARE WE BORN AGAIN INTO THE KINGDOM OF GOD A NEW CREATION.

"THEREFORE, IF ANY MAN IS IN CHRIST, <u>HE IS A NEW CREATION</u>. THE OLD THINGS PASSED AWAY, BEHOLD ALL THINGS BECOME NEW." (II CORINTHIANS 5:17)

"FOR CHRIST ALSO DIED FOR SINS <u>ONCE FOR ALL</u>, THE JUST FOR THE UNJUST, IN ORDER THAT HE MIGHT BRING US TO

GOD, HAVING BEEN PUT TO DEATH IN THE FLESH, BUT MADE ALIVE IN THE SPIRIT; AND CORRESPONDING TO THAT, BAPTISM NOW SAVES YOU . . . NOT THE REMOVAL OF DIRT FROM THE FLESH, BUT AN APPEAL TO GOD FOR A GOOD CONSCIENCE---THROUGH THE RESURRECTION OF JESUS CHRIST." (I PETER 3:17 & 21)

IN ACTS 2:38, HE GAVE SPECIFIC INSTRUCTIONS THROUGH PETER TO BE WATER BAPTIZED IN HIS NAME. MANY BELIEVE THAT WATER BAPTISM IS NOT IMPORTANT, AND WE CAN BE SAVED AND GO TO HEAVEN BY SIMPLY ACCEPTING HIM AS OUR SAVIOR. BUT WE MUST BE FILLED WITH HIS POWER TO OVERCOME THINGS THAT COME AGAINST US IN THIS LIFE HERE ON EARTH. BY NOT FOLLOWING HIS WAY OF DOING THINGS IT WILL ALMOST ALWAYS RESULT IN OUR FALLING BACK INTO OUR OLD WAYS AND MAY EVENTUALLY COST US OUR SALVATION AND ETERNITY IN HEAVEN.

HE REQUIRES US TO FOLLOW HIM IN THE WATERS OF BAPTISM. SO THAT IS WHAT WE MUST DO. JESUS, HIMSELF WAS BAPTIZED IN THE JORDAN RIVER BY JOHN THE BAPTIST, AND WE ARE COMMANDED TO FOLLOW HIS EXAMPLE. (MATTHEW 3:13-16) "THEN JESUS ARRIVED FROM GALILEE AT THE JORDAN COMING TO JOHN TO BE BAPTIZED BY HIM. BUT JOHN TRIED TO PREVENT HIM SAYING, 'I

HAVE NEED TO BE BAPTIZED BY YOU, AND DO YOU COME TO ME?'

"BUT JESUS ANSWERING SAID TO HIM, 'PERMIT IT AT THIS TIME, FOR IN THIS WAY IT IS FITTING FOR US TO FULFILL ALL RIGHTEOUSNESS.' THEN HE PERMITTED (OR BAPTIZED) HIM.

"AND AFTER BEING BAPTIZED, JESUS WENT UP IMMEDIATELY FROM THE WATER; AND BEHOLD THE HEAVENS WERE OPENED, AND HE SAW THE SPIRIT OF GOD DESCENDING AS A DOVE AND COMING UPON HIM."

SO, WE SEE HERE THAT JESUS WAS FIRST BAPTIZED IN WATER, AND THEN HE WAS BAPTIZED IN THE HOLY SPIRIT. IF HE WAS REQUIRED TO DO THAT AS AN EXAMPLE FOR US TO FOLLOW, CAN WE DO ANY LESS?

THERE IS MUCH CONTROVERSY IN CHURCHES TODAY OVER BEING BAPTIZED IN THE NAME OF THE FATHER, SON AND HOLY SPIRIT VS BEING BAPTIZED IN THE NAME OF JESUS CHRIST. EITHER WAY YOU ARE BAPTIZED; IT WILL NOT MAKE A DIFFERENCE IN YOUR SALVATION. IF YOU ARE BAPTIZED OUT OF THE DEPTHS OF YOUR HEART TO FOLLOW JESUS, THAT IS ALL THAT MATTERS.

I WOULD LIKE TO SUGGEST, HOWEVER, THAT THE WORD OF GOD POINTS TO THE

FACT THAT THE WAY TO BE BAPTIZED IS IN THE NAME OF JESUS CHRIST. SO LET'S LOOK AT ACTS 2:38 AGAIN.

"AND PETER SAID, 'REPENT, AND LET EACH OF YOU BE BAPTIZED <u>IN THE NAME OF JESUS CHRIST</u> FOR THE FORGIVENESS OF YOUR SINS; AND YOU SHALL RECEIVE THE GIFT OF THE HOLY SPIRIT.'"

IT IS PLAIN TO SEE THAT IT SAYS NOTHING HERE ABOUT BEING BAPTIZED IN THE NAME OF THE FATHER, THE SON AND THE HOLY SPIRIT. IT TELLS US TO BE BAPTIZED <u>IN THE NAME OF JESUS CHRIST</u>.

HAVE YOU EVER STOPPED TO THINK THAT IN ALL OF THE COUNTRIES OF THE WORLD WHO WORSHIP OTHER GODS, ALL OF THEIR GODS HAVE NAMES? TWO OF THEM THAT COME TO MIND ARE "BUDDHA" AND "MOHAMMED". ALL OF THE ANCIENT GREEK GODS HAD NAMES. IN THE OLD TESTAMENT, YOU CAN FIND ACCOUNTS OF SEVERAL GODS THAT WERE WORSHIPPED, AND THEY ALL HAD NAMES.

OUR GOD HAS A NAME TOO. JOHN 17: 11-12 SHOWS US WHAT GOD'S NAME IS. "HOLY FATHER, KEEP THEM IN **THY** NAME, **THE NAME WHICH THOU HAST GIVEN ME** THAT THEY MAY BE ONE EVEN AS WE ARE. WHILE

I WAS WITH THEM I WAS KEEPING THEM IN **THY** NAME, **WHICH THOU HAST GIVEN ME**."

JESUS STATED VERY CLEARY THAT HE WAS KEEPING THE ONES THAT HAD ACCEPTED HIM IN HIS FATHER'S NAME, WHICH IS THE SAME NAME THAT HIS FATHER HAD GIVEN HIM. THEREFORE IT IS CLEAR HERE IN THE BIBLE THAT OUR GOD'S NAME IS "**JESUS**".

"THEREFORE, ALSO GOD HIGHLY EXALTED HIM (JESUS) AND BESTOWED ON HIM THE NAME WHICH IS ABOVE EVERY NAME, THAT AT THE NAME OF JESUS EVERY KNEE SHOULD BOW OF THOSE WHO ARE IN HEAVEN, AND ON EARTH AND UNDER THE EARTH (IN HELL), AND THAT EVERY TONGUE SHOULD CONFESS THAT JESUS CHRIST IS LORD, TO THE GLORY OF GOD THE FATHER." (PHILIPPIANS 2: 9-11)

(I MIGHT ADD HERE THAT EVERY KNEE MEANS EVERY KNEE. THOSE WHO DON'T BELIEVE AND ACCEPT HIM HERE ON EARTH, WILL ONE DAY BOW THEIR KNEE TO HIM AND DECLARE THAT HE IS INDEED LORD. SO, IT WOULD BE BETTER TO DO THAT NOW THAN LATER, DON'T YOU THINK?)

REMEMBER IN THE BEGINNING OF THIS BOOK WE SAW THAT II CORINTHIANS 13:1 SAID, "EVERY FACT IS TO BE CONFIRMED BY THE TESTIMONY OF TWO OR THREE WITNESSES."

FOUR TIMES IN THE NEW TESTAMENT IN THE BOOK OF ACTS, WE ARE TOLD TO BE BAPTIZED <u>IN THE NAME OF JESUS</u>. (ACTS 2:38; ACTS 8:16; ACTS 10:48 AND ACTS 19:5)

ONLY ONCE IN THE WHOLE BIBLE DID JESUS SAY TO BE BAPTIZED IN THE NAME OF THE FATHER, THE SON AND THE HOLY SPIRIT. (MATTHEW 28:19)

NOTICE THE WORD "NAME". IT IS SINGULAR, "NAME" NOT PLURAL "NAMES". IT IS VERY CLEAR HERE THAT HE IS SPEAKING OF <u>ONE NAME</u>, NOT THREE. THE WORD "FATHER" IS NOT A NAME. IT IS A TITLE. THE WORD "SON" IS NOT A NAME. IT IS A TITLE. THE WORDS "HOLY SPIRIT" ARE NOT NAMES. THEY ARE A TITLE.

GOD IS ONE: (JOHN 10:30) HE HAS A NAME. HIS NAME IS JESUS. WE SHOULD BE BAPTIZED IN HIS <u>NAME</u> NOT HIS <u>TITLES</u>. ONCE AGAIN, I WANT TO MAKE IT CLEAR THAT IF YOU HAVE NOT BEEN BAPTIZED IN HIS NAME YOU WILL NOT GO TO HELL!! WE ARE RESPONSIBLE TO ACCEPT JESUS AS OUR LORD AND SAVIOR AND TO FOLLOW HIS WORD TO THE BEST OF OUR ABILITY AS INDIVIDUALS. HOWEVER, IF WE SEE A REVELATION OF HIS NAME AND THE IMPORTANCE OF THE NAME OF JESUS, THEN IT MAKES GOOD SENSE TO BE BAPTIZED IN THE NAME OF JESUS IF AT ALL POSSIBLE.

ANOTHER SCRIPTURE THAT GOES ALONG WITH THIS IS: COLOSSIANS 3:17, "AND WHATEVER YOU DO IN WORD OR **DEED** (BAPTISM IS A DEED) DO ALL IN THE NAME OF JESUS CHRIST, GIVING THANKS THROUGH HIM TO GOD, THE FATHER." SO LET'S EXAMINE THIS VERSE OF SCRIPTURE MORE CAREFULLY TO DETERMINE WHAT JESUS MEANT WHEN HE SAID TO BE BAPTIZED IN THE NAME OF THE FATHER, SON AND HOLY SPIRIT.

NOW WE WILL EXAMINE THE WORD "BAPTIZE". IT COMES FROM THE GREEK WORD WHICH MEANS TO <u>DIP</u> OR <u>SUBMERSE</u>. NO WHERE IN THE WORD OF GOD DOES IT SAY TO "SPRINKLE" ANYONE. IT SAYS TO DIP OR SUBMERSE IN THE NAME OF JESUS CHRIST **FOUR** TIMES. THIS MEANS WE ARE TO GO ALL THE WAY UNDER THE WATER, NOT JUST BE "SPRINKLED."

ROMANS-6:4 STATES THAT WE ARE TO BE BURIED WITH HIM IN BAPTISM AND RAISED TO NEWNESS OF LIFE. WHEN SOMEONE IS BURIED, WE DO NOT "SPRINKLE" A LITTLE DIRT OVER THEM AND CONSIDER THEM BURIED. WE COMPLETELY "SUBMERSE" THEM IN THE GROUND AND COVER THEM OVER WITH DIRT.

IT IS THE SAME WITH WATER BAPTISM. WE MUST BE COMPLETELY SUBMERSED AND COVERED OVER WITH WATER. ONLY

THEN ARE WE TRULY "BURIED" WITH HIM IN BAPTISM. OUR SINS ARE SYMBOLICALLY WASHED AWAY IN THE WATER AND WE COME UP OUT OF THE WATER A NEW CREATION. (II CORINTHIANS 5:17)

WHEN WE FOLLOW HIS WORD IN OBEDIENCE HE MEETS US. HE WILL MEET YOU WHEN YOU COME UP OUT OF THE WATER. YOU WILL FEEL CLEAN INSIDE AND YOU WILL FEEL HIS PRESENCE.

THIS ALL LEADS US TO AN IMPORTANT QUESTION. <u>WHAT ABOUT BAPTIZING BABIES</u>? THERE IS NOWHERE IN THE WORD OF GOD THAT COMMANDS US TO BAPTIZE BABIES. IN EVERY INSTANCE, THE WORD OF GOD SHOWS US THAT THOSE WHO WERE BAPTIZED WERE PEOPLE WHO HAD COME TO THE REALIZATION THAT THEY NEEDED TO BE "BORN AGAIN" AND THAT THEY NEEDED A SAVIOR. THEY WERE ALL OF AN AGE TO BE ABLE TO CHOOSE FOR THEMSELVES. BABIES CANNOT CHOOSE. REMEMBER, GOD REQUIRES US TO CHOOSE HIM. IT IS NOT MANDATORY.

AS PARENTS, WE CAN DEDICATE OUR BABIES TO GOD. WE CAN SEE THAT THEY ARE FULLY EQUIPPED WITH THE WORD OF GOD FROM BIRTH UNTIL THEY ARE ABLE TO MAKE THAT DECISION ON THEIR OWN. WE CAN AND SHOULD LIVE GODLY LIVES BEFORE THEM TO SHOW THEM THE KINGDOM OF GOD

THROUGH OUR BELIEFS AND ACTIONS. BUT, WE CANNOT CHOOSE WHETHER THEY WILL SERVE GOD ONCE THEY HAVE REACHED THE AGE OF ACCOUNTABILITY. EACH PERSON ON THIS EARTH HAS TO MAKE THAT CHOICE FOR THEMSELVES. JAMES 4:8 SAYS, "DRAW NEAR TO GOD, AND HE WILL DRAW NEAR TO YOU."

JOHN THE BAPTIST WAS THE FIRST PERSON TO SHOW PEOPLE ON EARTH WHAT GOD REQUIRED OF THEM REGARDING BAPTISM. BEFORE THAT THE CHILDREN OF GOD WERE UNDER LAWS GIVEN TO MEN AND WOMEN TO BRING THEIR BABIES TO THE TEMPLE AND DEDICATE THEM TO GOD.

JESUS WAS NO EXCEPTION. HIS PARENTS BROUGHT HIM TO THE TEMPLE TO BE DEDICATED WHEN HE WAS ONLY A FEW DAYS OLD. WE SEE THE ACCOUNT OF IT IN LUKE 2:22-39.

JESUS HIMSELF WAS NOT BAPTIZED UNTIL HE WAS OLDER. REMEMBER IN MATTHEW 3:13-16, HE CAME TO JOHN THE BAPTIST TO BE BAPTIZED WHEN HE WAS READY TO BEGIN HIS MINISTRY HERE ON EARTH. JESUS CAME TO JOHN TO BE BAPTIZED PUBLICALLY TO BE THE EXAMPLE FOR US TO FOLLOW. SO, AS BORN AGAIN BELIEVERS, WE ARE TO DO THE SAME.

NOW THAT WE HAVE BEEN BORN OF THE WATER, WE MUST BE BORN OF THE SPIRIT. ACCORDING TO ACTS 2:38 WHEN WE FOLLOW THE LORD IN WATER BAPTISM, HE PROMISES TO GIVE US THE GIFT OF THE HOLY SPIRIT. NOT ONLY THAT, BUT HE PROMISES US IN VERSE 39 THAT IT IS NOT ONLY FOR US, BUT FOR OUR CHILDREN AND ALL WHO THE LORD CALLS THROUGH US. SO LET'S SEE HOW TO RECEIVE HIS GIFT OF THE HOLY SPIRIT!

HOW IS MAN BORN OF THE SPIRIT?

IF THE NEWBORN BABY DOESN'T TAKE A BREATH OF AIR AND START BREATHING ON ITS OWN, IT WILL NOT LIVE. IT IS JUST AS VITALLY IMPORTANT FOR US ONCE WE HAVE BEEN CLEANSED IN WATER BAPTISM AND GIVEN NEW LIFE, TO GET OUR "BREATH OF AIR" AND BE BAPTIZED IN OUR SPIRITS WITH A SECOND BAPTISM, WHICH IS THE BAPTISM OF THE HOLY SPIRIT. WE MUST HAVE THE "BREATH" OF THE HOLY SPIRIT RESIDING IN US TO GUIDE, DIRECT AND MATURE US THROUGHOUT OUR LIVES.

ONE OF THE MOST CONTROVERSIAL ISSUES IN THE CHURCH WORLD TODAY IS THE HOLY SPIRIT. WHO IS THE HOLY SPIRIT? HOW DO YOU GET THE HOLY SPIRIT? HOW DO YOU KNOW YOU HAVE THE HOLY SPIRIT? IS THE HOLY SPIRIT FOR THE CHURCH TODAY, OR WAS HE ONLY FOR THE EARLY CHURCH? DO YOU HAVE TO SPEAK IN TONGUES?

THERE IS ONLY ONE WAY TO SETTLE THE ISSUE. WE MUST GO TO THE WORD OF GOD AND FIND OUR ANSWERS. WE CANNOT TAKE MAN'S VIEWS ON AN ISSUE AS IMPORTANT AS THIS ONE.

FIRST, WE MUST ESTABLISH THE FACT THAT THE HOLY SPIRIT IS GOD. HE IS AS MUCH GOD AS THE FATHER AND THE SON ARE. WE CAN SEE THIS IN MATTHEW 28:19 "GO THEREFORE AND MAKE DISCIPLES OF ALL NATIONS, BAPTIZING THEM IN THE NAME OF THE FATHER AND THE SON AND THE HOLY SPIRIT. IT IS PLAIN TO SEE FROM THIS SCRIPTURE THAT THE HOLY SPIRIT IS CONSIDERED EQUAL WITH THE FATHER AND THE SON.

JOHN 14:26 TELLS US WHO THE HOLY SPIRIT IS AND WHY IT IS IMPORTANT TO HAVE HIM LIVING INSIDE OF US. "BUT THE HELPER, THE HOLY SPIRIT, WHOM THE FATHER WILL SEND IN MY NAME, HE WILL TEACH YOU ALL THINGS AND BRING TO YOUR REMEMBRANCE ALL THAT I SAID TO YOU."

II CORINTHIANS 13:14 STATES; "THE GRACE OF THE LORD JESUS CHRIST, AND THE LOVE OF GOD, AND THE **FELLOWSHIP OF THE HOLY SPIRIT** BE WITH YOU ALL." JUST THINK OF THAT!!! GOD STILL WANTS TO FELLOWSHIP WITH MANKIND, AND HE COMES TO EARTH,

HIMSELF IN THE FORM OF THE HOLY SPIRIT TO DO THAT.

"BUT IF THE SPIRIT OF HIM WHO RAISED JESUS FROM THE DEAD DWELLS IN YOU, HE WHO RAISED CHRIST JESUS FROM THE DEAD WILL ALSO GIVE LIFE TO YOUR MORTAL BODIES **THROUGH HIS SPIRIT WHO INDWELLS YOU**." ROMANS 8:8-11.

IT IS THE HOLY SPIRIT THAT GIVES US LIFE AND LIGHT AND MAKES THE GLORIOUS WORD OF GOD COME ALIVE. IN ORDER TO SEE OR UNDERSTAND THE KINGDOM OF GOD, AND THE WORD OF GOD, WE MUST HAVE THE BAPTISM OF THE HOLY SPIRIT AS WELL AS BAPTISM IN WATER.

IN ORDER TO MORE FULLY UNDERSTAND THE BAPTISM IN THE HOLY SPIRIT, WE MUST STUDY IT IN MORE DETAIL. THE WORD OF GOD STATES THAT GOD DOES NOT CHANGE, BUT HE IS THE SAME YESTERDAY, TODAY AND FOREVER. (MALACHI 3:6; HEBREWS 13:8)

GOING BACK TO ACTS 2:38 AGAIN, WE READ THAT ONCE WE HAVE REPENTED AND BEEN WATER BAPTIZED WE **SHALL** RECEIVE THE **GIFT** OF THE HOLY SPIRIT. IF HE REQUIRES US TO BE BAPTIZED IN HIS NAME FOR THE FORGIVENESS OF OUR SINS, WHY WOULDN'T HE REQUIRE HIS BORN AGAIN BELIEVERS TO RECEIVE HIS **GIFT** OF THE HOLY SPIRIT?

THE HOLY SPIRIT IS HIS GIFT TO US IF WE ARE BORN AGAIN! ACTS 2:38 SAYS SO! WHAT DO WE HAVE TO DO TO RECEIVE A GIFT? THE ANSWER IS VERY SIMPLE. **JUST RECEIVE IT**! JUST BELIEVE WHAT HIS WORD SAYS TO YOU AND IN HIS TIME AND IN HIS WAY HE WILL GIVE IT TO YOU. REMEMBER, IT IS GOD WHO REQUIRES US TO HAVE HIS GIFT. (JOHN 3:3-5) THEREFORE, IF IT IS HIS REQUIREMENT, THEN IT IS UP TO HIM TO GIVE IT TO US.

JESUS WAS OUR PATTERN TO FOLLOW. HE WAS THE FIRST BORN AGAIN MAN. AFTER HE WAS BAPTIZED, HE RECEIVED THE GIFT OF THE HOLY SPIRIT. JOHN THE BAPTIST SAW THE HOLY SPIRIT DESCENDING FROM HEAVEN IN THE FORM OF A DOVE. (LUKE 3:21; MARK 1:10; MATTHEW 3:16) AS DISCIPLES OF JESUS, WE ARE TO FOLLOW THE EXAMPLES THAT HE SET FOR US IN THE NEW TESTAMENT. WE TOO ARE TO RECEIVE THE GIFT OF THE HOLY SPIRIT.

SO, WHY DO WE NEED THE GIFT OF THE HOLY SPIRIT? "YOU SHALL RECEIVE **POWER** WHEN THE HOLY SPIRIT HAS COME UPON YOU". (ACTS 1:8; EPHESIANS 3:16) WE NEED THE **POWER** OF THE HOLY SPIRIT TO SEE THE REVELATION OF GOD'S WORD. WE NEED THE **POWER** OF THE HOLY SPIRIT TO STAND AGAINST THE CROWD AND BE SEPARATE TO FOLLOW THE WORD OF GOD RATHER THAN THE PEOPLE IN THE WORLD. WE NEED THE **POWER** OF THE HOLY SPIRIT TO SAY "NO" AND

TO MEAN IT. OUR CHILDREN NEED THE POWER OF THE HOLY SPIRIT TO STAND AGAINST THE TEMPTATIONS AND PEER PRESSURES THAT ARE ALL AROUND THEM TODAY. WE NEED THE **POWER** OF THE HOLY SPIRIT TO OVERCOME THE FORCES THAT COME AGAINST US. TO HE WHO OVERCOMES WILL JESUS GRANT THE KINGDOM OF GOD (REVELATION 2:7; 17 & 26; REVELATION 3:5, 12 & 21)

THAT IS WHY WE NEED THE HOLY SPIRIT. WE MUST HAVE THE POWER TO OVERCOME ALL THE THINGS WITHIN US AND OUTSIDE OF US UNTIL WE COME INTO THE IMAGE OF JESUS CHRIST UNTO A MATURE MAN. (ROMANS 8:29; I CORINTHIANS 15:49; PHILIPPIANS 3:21; EPHESIANS 4:13; I CORINTHIANS 14:20; COLOSSIANS 1: 28-29)

PAUL SAID IN COLOSSIANS 1:29 THAT HE WAS STRIVING ACCORDING TO HIS (JESUS') POWER WHICH MIGHTILY WORKED WITHIN HIM. WHAT POWER DID HE MEAN? IT WAS THE POWER OF THE HOLY SPIRIT.

MAN CANNOT DO THE WILL OF GOD BY HIS OWN POWER. THE HOLY SPIRIT IS THE PART OF GOD THAT IS SENT TO DWELL WITHIN US TO GIVE US THE POWER TO LIVE AS GOD DESIRES US TO. WE SEE THIS IN JOHN 14:16-17. "AND I WILL ASK THE FATHER, AND HE WILL GIVE YOU ANOTHER **HELPER**, THAT HE MAY BE WITH YOU FOREVER; THAT IS THE SPIRIT

OF TRUTH (THE HOLY SPIRIT) WHOM THE WORLD CANNOT RECEIVE BECAUSE IT DOES NOT BEHOLD HIM OR KNOW HIM. BUT YOU KNOW HIM BECAUSE HE ABIDES WITH YOU, **AND WILL BE IN YOU**."

THE GREEK WORD FOR "CHRIST" IS "ANOINTED". HIS ANOINTING MUST LIVE WITHIN YOU. MANY TIMES IN THE WORD OF GOD, JESUS SPOKE OF DWELLING IN US BY HIS SPIRIT. (JOHN 14:16-20; 23; 26; JOHN 15:26; COLOSSIANS 1:27)

AS WE JUST SAW, JESUS CALLS THE HOLY SPIRIT THE SPIRIT OF TRUTH IN JOHN 14:17. WE MUST HAVE THE TRUTH IN THESE DAYS, NOT MAN'S INTERPRETATION OF TRUTH. IT IS THE TRUTH THAT SETS US FREE. (JOHN 8:32) JESUS SAID HE IS THE WAY, THE TRUTH AND THE LIFE. (JOHN 14:6) JESUS WAS THE TRUTH AND THE HOLY SPIRIT IS CALLED THE SPIRIT OF TRUTH. THE SAME SPIRIT THAT RAISED CHRIST FROM THE DEAD DWELLS IN YOU. (ROMANS 8:11) THIS SPIRIT OF TRUTH WILL TEACH YOU ALL THINGS PERTAINING TO THE TRUTH FOUND IN GOD'S WORD. (JOHN 14:26; JOHN 16:13-15; I JOHN 2:20; 27)

WHY DO WE NEED THE SPIRIT OF TRUTH? "FOR EVEN SATAN DISGUISES HIMSELF AS AN ANGEL OF LIGHT": (II CORINTHIANS 11:14) ANOTHER WORD FOR "LIGHT" IS "TRUTH". HE DISGUISES HIMSELF AS THE TRUTH AND

THE WORD SAYS HE COMES IN THESE DAYS TO DECEIVE EVEN THE ELECT, THE ONES WHO HAVE ACCEPTED JESUS AS THEIR SAVIOR.

"FOR FALSE CHRIST'S AND FALSE PROPHETS WILL ARISE AND WILL SHOW GREAT SIGNS AND WONDERS, SO AS TO MISLEAD, IF POSSIBLE, EVEN THE <u>ELECT</u>." (MATTHEW 24:24) IF YOU ARE BORN AGAIN, YOU ARE THE <u>ELECT</u> OF GOD.

THOSE WHO DO NOT THINK IT IS NECESSARY TO HAVE THE HOLY SPIRIT LIVING IN THEM IN THE FULLNESS ARE BEING DECEIVED BY SATAN AND WILL EVENTUALLY BE LED INTO UNTRUTH. WE MUST HAVE THE SPIRIT OF TRUTH (THE HOLY SPIRIT) DWELLING AND LIVING IN US.

SO, HOW DO WE EXPERIENCE THE BAPTISM OF THE HOLY SPIRIT; AND HOW DO WE KNOW WE HAVE THE HOLY SPIRIT DWELLING IN US?

FIRST OF ALL, WE BELIEVE THE WORD OF GOD. ACTS 2:38 STATES THAT YOU **SHALL** RECEIVE THE GIFT OF THE HOLY SPIRIT ONCE YOU ARE BORN AGAIN. SO WE NEED TO BELIEVE THAT.

NEXT, YOU ASK GOD FOR IT. THIS IS ACCORDING TO THE WORD OF GOD: "ASK, AND IT SHALL BE GIVEN TO YOU; SEEK, AND YOU SHALL FIND, KNOCK AND IT SHALL BE

OPENED TO YOU. FOR EVERYONE WHO ASKS RECEIVES, AND HE WHO SEEKS FINDS, AND TO HIM WHO KNOCKS IT SHALL BE OPENED. OR WHAT MAN IS THERE AMONG YOU, WHEN HIS SON SHALL ASK HIM FOR A LOAF, WILL GIVE HIM A STONE? OR IF HE SHALL ASK FOR A FISH, HE WILL NOT GIVE HIM A SNAKE, WILL HE? IF YOU THEN BEING EVIL KNOW HOW TO GIVE GOOD GIFTS TO YOUR CHILDREN, HOW MUCH MORE SHALL YOUR HEAVENLY FATHER GIVE THE HOLY SPIRIT TO THOSE WHO ASK HIM?" (LUKE 11: 9-13)

YOU CAN OPEN YOUR HEART TO THE HOLY SPIRIT, INVITING HIM TO DWELL WITHIN YOU AND TO CONFORM YOU INTO HIS IMAGE AND THE DESIRES HE HAS FOR YOUR LIFE. TALK WITH HIM. HE LOVES YOU. WORSHIP HIM. THANK HIM. PRAISE HIM. GOD INHABITS THE PRAISES OF HIS PEOPLE. (PSALM 22:3) WHEN GOD BAPTIZES YOU WITH THE HOLY SPIRIT, YOU WILL EXPERIENCE A BEAUTIFUL UNION WITH HIM. YOU WILL FEEL HIS PRESENCE WITHIN YOU. THIS IS A SUPERNATURAL EXPERIENCE; AND ONCE YOU HAVE EXPERIENCED IT, YOU WILL NEVER BE ABLE TO FORGET IT. BESIDES THAT, YOU WILL FEEL IT FOR THE REST OF YOUR LIFE IF YOU CONTINUE TO FELLOWSHIP WITH GOD.

ACCORDING TO II CORINTHIANS 13:5, **JESUS CHRIST IS IN YOU**. HE IS IN YOU BY HIS SPIRIT IF YOU ARE BORN AGAIN. GOD THE FATHER,

JESUS THE SON AND THE HOLY SPIRIT ARE ONE ENTITY. "BUT IF THE SPIRIT OF HIM WHO RAISED JESUS FROM THE DEAD DWELLS IN YOU, HE WHO RAISED CHRIST JESUS FROM THE DEAD WILL ALSO GIVE LIFE TO YOUR MORTAL BODIES THROUGH HIS SPIRIT WHO INDWELLS YOU." (ROMANS 8:11)

THE EVIDENCE THAT YOU HAVE THE HOLY SPIRIT WITHIN YOU IS THE ABILITY TO SPEAK IN AN UNKNOWN, HEAVENLY LANGUAGE. THIS LANGUAGE IS ALSO KNOWN AS "TONGUES". YOU WILL NOT BE ABLE TO UNDERSTAND WHAT YOU ARE SPEAKING WITH YOUR NATURAL MIND. YOU WILL BE SPEAKING DIRECTLY TO THE THRONE OF GOD IN A LANGUAGE HE CAN UNDERSTAND. IT IS THE HOLY SPIRIT WITHIN YOU TALKING WITH THE FATHER IN HEAVEN ON YOUR BEHALF OR ON THE BEHALF OF SOMEONE ELSE.

ONE THING WE ALL NEED TO UNDERSTAND ABOUT PRAYING. GOD REQUIRES US TO PRAY AND ASK HIM FOR OURSELVES AND FOR OTHER PEOPLE. GOD GAVE THE EARTH TO MAN. HE SELDOM ACTS APART FROM THE PRAYERS OF HIS PEOPLE HERE ON EARTH. HE ALSO ONLY ACTS ON HIS WORD! THAT IS A VERY IMPORTANT POINT TO UNDERSTAND. GOD DOESN'T ACT ON OUR WORDS. HE ACTS ON HIS WORDS. WE NEED TO PRAY AND ASK ACCORDING TO HIS WILL; AND HIS WORD IS HIS WILL. WHEN WE PRAY IN AN UNKNOWN

TONGUE, WE CAN KNOW WE ARE PRAYING ACCORDING TO HIS WILL EVERY TIME.

I CORINTHIANS 14:14 SAYS, "FOR IF I PRAY IN A TONGUE, MY SPIRIT PRAYS, BUT MY MIND IS UNFRUITFUL." SOMETIMES AT FIRST, YOU WILL ONLY GET A WORD OR TWO IN AN UNKNOWN LANGUAGE. JUST KEEP REPEATING THAT WORD OR TWO, KEEP PRAISING GOD AND LOVING HIM, AND BEFORE YOU KNOW IT, YOU WILL BE SPEAKING FLUENTLY; AND YOU WILL ALSO BE ABLE TO SING FLUENTLY IN THE HOLY SPIRIT.

READ THE 14TH CHAPTER OF I CORINTHIANS. DO NOT WORRY ABOUT PROPHESYING. THAT IS A DEEPER MANIFESTATION OF THE GIFT OF TONGUES. TAKE SPECIAL NOTICE THAT, "ONE WHO SPEAKS IN AN UNKNOWN TONGUE DOES NOT SPEAK TO MEN, BUT TO GOD; FOR NO ONE UNDERSTANDS, BUT IN HIS SPIRIT HE SPEAKS MYSTERIES." (VS 2) "ONE, WHO SPEAKS IN A TONGUE, EDIFIES HIMSELF." (VS. 4) THIS MEANS HE BUILDS HIMSELF UP. .. . "SO THEN TONGUES ARE FOR A <u>SIGN</u>, NOT TO THOSE WHO BELIEVE, <u>BUT TO UNBELIEVERS</u>." (VS. 22) "DO NOT FORBID TO SPEAK IN TONGUES." (VS 39)

ROMANS 8:26 SHOWS HOW THE HOLY SPIRIT INTERCEDES FOR US. WE DO NOT KNOW WHAT THE WILL OF GOD IS IN SOME INSTANCES. IF WE PRAY WITH THE HOLY SPIRIT IN OUR

HEAVENLY LANGUAGE, THE HOLY SPIRIT WITHIN US PRAYS ACCORDING TO THE WILL OF GOD NOT ACCORDING TO OUR CARNAL MIND. THIS IS A VERY IMPORTANT REASON WHY WE NEED THE HOLY SPIRIT DWELLING WITHIN US. WE THINK WE KNOW THE WAY THINGS SHOULD GO, BUT OUR HEAVENLY FATHER KNOWS WHAT IS BEST FOR US. WHEN WE PRAY IN HIS LANGUAGE, HE ANSWERS!

"BUT AN HOUR IS COMING, AND NOW IS, WHEN THE TRUE WORSHIPPERS SHALL WORSHIP THE FATHER IN SPIRIT AND TRUTH; FOR SUCH PEOPLE THE FATHER SEEKS TO BE HIS WORSHIPPERS. GOD IS SPIRIT; AND THOSE WHO WORSHIP HIM MUST WORSHIP IN SPIRIT AND IN TRUTH." (JOHN 4:23-24)

BELIEVE!   ASK!   RECEIVE!

THE HOLY SPIRIT IS GOD'S GIFT TO YOU!

CONCLUSION

THROUGHOUT THIS BOOK WE HAVE SEEN THAT MAN WAS ORIGINALLY CREATED IN THE IMAGE OF GOD; BUT BECAUSE ADAM CHOSE TO DISOBEY GOD, HE AND EVE DIED SPIRITUALLY AND GAVE THIS EARTH TO SATAN TO RULE OVER.

WE ALSO DISCOVERED WHAT HELL IS AND WHAT IT WOULD BE LIKE TO GO THERE IF WE DON'T ACCEPT JESUS AS OUR SAVIOR.

THEN WE SAW THAT GOD CAME HIMSELF IN THE FORM OF HIS SON, JESUS, AND DIED FOR MAN. HE THEN WENT TO HELL AND ROSE AGAIN BECAUSE HE WAS SINLESS. HE OVERCAME DEATH AND SATAN HAD NO LEGAL RIGHT TO KEEP HIM IN HELL. HE ROSE AND GAVE MAN A CHOICE ONCE AGAIN TO EITHER FOLLOW GOD OR SATAN.

HOW GREAT A LOVE OUR GOD HAS FOR THE MAN HE CREATED! OUR MINDS CANNOT EVEN COMPREHEND ALL THAT HE DID FOR US AND THE VAST, AWESOME LOVE HE HAS

FOR US, EVEN WHILE WE ARE YET IN SIN. **IT DOESN'T MATTER WHAT YOU HAVE DONE OR HOW BAD YOU ARE, JESUS DIED FOR YOU AND HE WILL FORGIVE YOU IF YOU ASK HIM TO**.

WE CAN NOW ACCEPT HIM AS OUR SAVIOR AND MAKE HIM LORD OF OUR LIVES. WHEN WE DECIDE TO MAKE HIM OUR SAVIOR, WE REPENT OF OUR SIN AND ASK HIM TO FORGIVE US. HE THEN FORGIVES US AND CLEANSES US FROM ALL THE PAST, MAKING US NEW CREATIONS IN CHRIST JESUS.

THEN AS WE FOLLOW ON TO MAKE HIM LORD OF OUR LIVES, WE READ HIS WORD, SEEKING TO KNOW HIM. WE FOLLOW HIM IN WATER BAPTISM, AND HE GIVES US HIS GIFT OF THE HOLY SPIRIT. HE COMES IN THE FORM OF THE HOLY SPIRIT AND LIVES INSIDE OUR SPIRITS, ENABLING US TO OVERCOME, AND GIVING US THE POWER TO LIVE FOR HIM.

HIS SPIRIT IN US OPENS OUR MINDS TO UNDERSTAND HIS WORD AND HIS GREAT LOVE FOR US. WE CAN BE ASSURED THAT WHEN WE LEAVE THIS EARTH, WE WILL GO TO HEAVEN TO LIVE ETERNALLY WITH HIM. WE CAN EXPERIENCE ALL THAT LOVE, JOY AND PEACE WE SO YEARN FOR HERE ON EARTH.

BECAUSE GOD SO LOVED US, JESUS TOOK OUR SINS UPON HIS OWN BODY FOR US. HE PAID THE PRICE WE WERE OBLIGATED TO PAY,

AND SET US FREE TO CHOOSE ETERNAL LIFE WITH HIM IN HEAVEN OR ETERNAL DEATH WITH SATAN IN HELL.

THE CHOICE IS NOW YOURS TO MAKE. WILL YOU CHOOSE ETERNAL LIFE OR ETERNAL DEATH?

IF YOU HAVEN'T GIVEN YOUR LIFE TO GOD YET AND YOU WANT TO DO SO, SAY THIS PRAYER NOW FROM YOUR HEART AND BEGIN TO LIVE ETERNALLY RIGHT THIS MINUTE IN HIM.

"FATHER, I BELIEVE THE WORDS IN THIS BOOK. I COME TO YOU IN THE NAME OF YOUR SON, JESUS.

I BELIEVE HE WAS BORN OF A VIRGIN; HE DIED FOR MY SINS AND ROSE AGAIN TO GIVE ME ETERNAL LIFE WITH YOU.
I ASK YOU TO FORGIVE ME FOR ALL MY SINS AND TO CLEANSE ME RIGHT NOW FROM EVERYTHING THAT IS NOT PLEASING TO YOU.

I CHOOSE TO TURN FROM MY PAST, FROM MY SINS, AND TO MAKE JESUS MY SAVIOR AND THE LORD OF MY LIFE.

PLEASE BAPTIZE ME WITH YOUR HOLY SPIRIT AS I FOLLOW YOU IN THE WATERS OF BAPTISM.

I ASK THAT YOU LIVE IN ME AND HELP ME TO LIVE FOR YOU. THANK YOU THAT ACCORDING TO YOUR WORD, I AM NOW BORN AGAIN AND WILL LIVE ETERNALLY WITH YOU.

I PRAY THESE THINGS IN THE NAME OF JESUS!
AMEN"

GOD BLESS YOU AS YOU SEEK HIM. MAY HE GIVE YOU ALL THE TRUTH, LOVE, JOY AND PEACE YOU ARE LOOKING FOR!

"PEACE BE WITH YOU, AND LOVE WITH FAITH, FROM GOD THE FATHER AND THE LORD JESUS CHRIST. AMEN" (EPHESIANS 6:23)

ABOUT THE AUTHOR

Sandra Taylor was born Sandra Ashton in Traverse City, Michigan on July 25, 1940. She was born again on January 7, 1976.

Growing up, she didn't know that Jesus was the Savior of the world. The little bit of church she did attend taught that God was love, but didn't put any emphasis on Jesus at all. So when she heard what Jesus did for her, it was all new and exciting.

From the minute she received Jesus as her Savior; she had a real thirst for knowledge of God and His word and studied the Bible extensively. God gave her revelation of His word and she began to write the things He showed her down; filling many notebooks with the things He showed her and the things she heard in church.

She didn't know it then, but God was developing a teaching gift in her. As she matured in the gift of teaching, she wanted to be able to explain to others what took place from the beginning of creation through how to be born again and what God required of those who follow Him. She looked for a book that explained it, but couldn't find one. So, she decided to write one herself. This book is the result of her quest.

She moved to Fort Worth, Texas in 1987. She attended Bible School for a time and continued to grow and mature in the word of God. In 1997 she married Glenn Taylor. Glenn had the heart of an evangelist. In November, 2000 God put a call upon Glenn to visit a man on Texas Death Row who was soon to be executed. When Glenn got in to see him, the man was aglow with the Holy Spirit. He had repented and turned his life over to the Lord and was eager to leave this world and meet Jesus in heaven.

On the way home, Glenn asked the Lord why He had sent him there since the man was already born again and clearly ready to be with Jesus. God spoke back to him that this was to be his ministry from now on. He also told him that He wanted those on Death Row to leave this world just like that man. . . filled with the Holy Spirit and eager to see Jesus.

As a result, JLM Prison Ministries was birthed. The teachings that Sandra had recorded were soon put into a monthly newsletter titled "Notes From Mom".

Sandra was ordained in February, 2002. Glenn passed away in January, 2009 and Sandra carries on the ministry to this day. As of the writing of this book, there are over 200 inmates on the mailing list for the Newsletter. Sandra also corresponds with many inmates and their family members, sends Bibles in to inmates and sends a Bible Study in to any who want it.

To contact Sandra you can write to JLM Prison Ministries, P.O. Box 48123, Watauga, TX 76148. You can also visit the website for some of her "Notes from Mom", stories of the miraculous salvations she and Glenn have seen, and much more at: jlmministries.com.